Social Security

Other Books in the Current Controversies Series

| Social Security

Debra A. Miller, Book Editor

GREENHAVEN PRESS
A part of Gale, Cengage Learning

GALE
CENGAGE Learning·

Detroit • New York • San Francisco • New Haven, Conn • Waterville, Maine • London

GALE
CENGAGE Learning·

Elizabeth Des Chenes, *Director, Content Strategy*
Cynthia Sanner, *Publisher*
Douglas Dentino, *Manager, New Product*

For more information, contact:
Greenhaven Press
27500 Drake Rd.
Farmington Hills, MI 48331-3535
Or you can visit our Internet site at gale.cengage.com

Cover image © Kim Reinick/Shutterstock.com.

LIBRARY OF CONGRESS CATALOGING-IN-PUBLICATION DATA

Social security / Debra A. Miller, book editor.
p. cm. -- (Current controversies)
Includes bibliographical references and index.
ISBN 978-0-7377-6245-7 (hardcover) -- ISBN 978-0-7377-6246-4 (pbk.)
1. Social security--United States. I. Miller, Debra A.
HD7125.S5924 2013
368.4'300973--dc23
                                                    2012050513

Printed in the United States of America
1 2 3 4 5 6 7 17 16 15 14 13

Contents

Social Security showed a $2.7 trillion surplus at the end of 2011. Projected benefit cuts in 2033 can be avoided through a combination of policy changes, such as increasing the income cap on which Social Security taxes apply, and improvements in the US economy.

Chapter 2: Is Social Security a Successful Government Program?

Ponzi scheme or not, Social Security will not be able to pay today's level of benefits to future retirees. Current workers should prepare for this shortfall, and there are four ways to do so.

Chapter 3: Would Private Retirement Accounts Be Better than the Current System?

Yes: Private Retirement Accounts Would Be Better than the Current Social Security System

President Barack Obama has called Republican proposals for private Social Security accounts ill-conceived. But even if invested conservatively, private accounts would give workers much higher returns than Social Security. People should have the choice to participate in Social Security or to invest that amount of their earnings in privately controlled investment accounts.

Chapter 4: How Should Social Security's Fiscal Issues Be Fixed?

Foreword

By definition, controversies are "discussions of questions in which opposing opinions clash" (*Webster's Twentieth Century Dictionary Unabridged*). Few would deny that controversies are a pervasive part of the human condition and exist on virtually every level of human enterprise. Controversies transpire between individuals and among groups, within nations and between nations. Controversies supply the grist necessary for progress by providing challenges and challengers to the status quo. They also create atmospheres where strife and warfare can flourish. A world without controversies would be a peaceful world; but it also would be, by and large, static and prosaic.

The Series' Purpose

The purpose of the Current Controversies series is to explore many of the social, political, and economic controversies dominating the national and international scenes today. Titles selected for inclusion in the series are highly focused and specific. For example, from the larger category of criminal justice, Current Controversies deals with specific topics such as police brutality, gun control, white collar crime, and others. The debates in Current Controversies also are presented in a useful, timeless fashion. Articles and book excerpts included in each title are selected if they contribute valuable, long-range ideas to the overall debate. And wherever possible, current information is enhanced with historical documents and other relevant materials. Thus, while individual titles are current in focus, every effort is made to ensure that they will not become quickly outdated. Books in the Current Controversies series will remain important resources for librarians, teachers, and students for many years.

In addition to keeping the titles focused and specific, great care is taken in the editorial format of each book in the series. Book introductions and chapter prefaces are offered to provide background material for readers. Chapters are organized around several key questions that are answered with diverse opinions representing all points on the political spectrum. Materials in each chapter include opinions in which authors clearly disagree as well as alternative opinions in which authors may agree on a broader issue but disagree on the possible solutions. In this way, the content of each volume in Current Controversies mirrors the mosaic of opinions encountered in society. Readers will quickly realize that there are many viable answers to these complex issues. By questioning each author's conclusions, students and casual readers can begin to develop the critical thinking skills so important to evaluating opinionated material.

Current Controversies is also ideal for controlled research. Each anthology in the series is composed of primary sources taken from a wide gamut of informational categories including periodicals, newspapers, books, US and foreign government documents, and the publications of private and public organizations. Readers will find factual support for reports, debates, and research papers covering all areas of important issues. In addition, an annotated table of contents, an index, a book and periodical bibliography, and a list of organizations to contact are included in each book to expedite further research.

Perhaps more than ever before in history, people are confronted with diverse and contradictory information. During the Persian Gulf War, for example, the public was not only treated to minute-to-minute coverage of the war, it was also inundated with critiques of the coverage and countless analyses of the factors motivating US involvement. Being able to sort through the plethora of opinions accompanying today's major issues, and to draw one's own conclusions, can be a complicated and frustrating struggle. It is the editors' hope that Current Controversies will help readers with this struggle.

Introduction

> *"Franklin D. Roosevelt (1882–1945), who was elected president in 1932 during the Great Depression, made economic security a national priority, achieving passage in 1935 of his plan: the Social Security Act (SSA)."*

Before 1900, people who were ill, elderly, or unable to work relied on family, friends, or charity for help in order to survive, but as societies developed, providing economic security for older and disabled persons typically came to be understood as a governmental function. Many European countries adopted some form of social security during the late 1800s or early 1900s, long before US policymakers considered such a program. In the United States, the need for such a system became evident during the Great Depression of the 1930s—an unprecedented economic crisis that caused about 25 percent of the workforce to be out of work, overwhelmed charities, and left families suddenly without their bank-held savings and struggling to put food on the table and care for aged, sick, or disabled relatives. Franklin D. Roosevelt (1882–1945), who was elected president in 1932 during the Great Depression, made economic security a national priority, achieving passage in 1935 of his plan: the Social Security Act (SSA).

President Roosevelt began his push for a national plan for economic security in 1934 by creating the Committee on Economic Security (CES). This committee was charged with studying the need for social insurance for elderly and disabled Americans and making recommendations to the president and Congress. The CES assembled a team of experts, held town meetings to gather information from citizens, and considered

European social security models. In January 1935, the CES sent its report to the president, and Congress held hearings on its proposals. Legislation passed both houses of Congress by overwhelming majorities and was signed by the president on August 14, 1935.

The SSA created a social insurance program that paid retired workers aged sixty-five or older an income during their retirement. Initially, the program simply paid a lump sum to retirees, but beginning in 1940, it began paying out monthly benefits. The amount paid was based on the individual's payroll tax contributions to the program. The original SSA also contained the nation's first unemployment insurance program; aid to the states for various health and welfare programs; and the Aid to Dependent Children program, which provided financial assistance to children of single parents or whose families had low or no income. The act was intended to help ameliorate the problems associated with old age, poverty, unemployment, and the death of family breadwinners.

Since 1935, the Social Security Act has been amended several times. In 1939, the program was changed to add benefits for the spouse or minor children of retired workers and a survivor's benefit for families of workers who died prematurely. In 1950, the SSA was amended to provide cost of living adjustments (COLA) to Social Security benefits, with a 77 percent COLA authorized for 1950 and a second COLA of 12.5 percent set for 1952. In 1956, disability benefits were added to provide income for workers with disabilities so severe that they cannot work. Other significant changes included a 1961 amendment that provided for an early retirement age for men of sixty-two with a reduced monthly benefit, and a 1972 amendment that authorized a number of changes, including automatic COLAs, a maximum monthly benefit, increased benefits for workers who waited until age sixty-five to retire, and a system to periodically increase the amount of earnings subject to Social Security payroll taxes.

Over the years, Social Security has also been modified to avoid potential financial crises created by changing demographics, inadequate tax proceeds, and similar issues. In 1975, for example, when payroll taxes were projected to be insufficient to meet payouts by 1979, the Congress increased the payroll tax rate, reduced benefits, and made other fiscal changes. A similar problem was corrected in 1983 after President Ronald Reagan created the Greenspan Commission to study the issue: the president followed the committee's recommendations to make changes such as taxing some Social Security benefits, including federal employees in the payroll tax system, and increasing the retirement age for future workers. President George W. Bush also sought (but failed) to pass Social Security reforms after a 2005 Treasury Department report found that the program would be paying out more than it collected in taxes as of 2018.

In 2013, the Social Security system continued to face fiscal problems. With the large baby boomer generation beginning to retire, the system looked like it faced a shortfall. The trustees for the Social Security program reported in 2012 that it began running at a deficit in 2010 and that it could exhaust trust fund assets by 2033. Critics have also pointed out that the Social Security trust fund—a term used to refer to surplus tax collections garnered by the program—have been used as part of the general federal budget and that any current or future Social Security deficits must be paid by the federal government out of yearly government income or from money borrowed from other countries. The authors of the viewpoints included in *Current Controversies: Social Security* discuss the various issues arising from this current fiscal situation, including whether Social Security is going bankrupt, whether it is a successful government program, whether private retirement accounts would be a better retirement system for workers, and how the program's fiscal problems could be fixed.

CHAPTER 1

Is Social Security Going Bankrupt?

Chapter Preface

The Social Security program provides benefits for retired workers and their families; it also provides disability insurance that pays a monthly benefit to severely disabled workers who are no longer able to work. The insurance part of Social Security comprises two programs: Social Security Disability Insurance (SSDI) and Supplemental Security Income (SSI). Disability benefits, however, were not part of the original Social Security Act passed in 1935. They were added later after much congressional study and debate.

SSDI became part of the nation's economic security plan in August 1956. Unlike Social Security retirement insurance, the disability insurance was controversial. Much of the discussion about disability insurance prior to its passage concerned how much disability workers would need to have to qualify for benefits and whether the emphasis should rather be on rehabilitation than on paying income for life. Many people supported the idea of trying to help the disabled reach their maximum useful potential rather than allowing these individuals to become permanently dependent on the government. However, in 1956, Congress finally accepted the fact that many workers cannot be rehabilitated and some form of income support had to be provided for them. Still, the 1956 version of SSDI was limited to workers age fifty or older and did not include benefits for the dependents of disabled workers. Given the age limit, the program was restricted to people who typically have disabilities such as heart disease and arthritis that cannot be rehabilitated. Therefore, the SSDI program eventually lost its link to rehabilitation and became just another part of the Social Security retirement package.

The SSI program, the second part of the disability program, was enacted in 1972 as part of the welfare reform plan of President Richard Nixon (1913–1994). At this time, adult federal welfare programs that provided benefits to low and no income persons—such as Aid to the Blind, Aid to the Permanently and Totally Disabled, and Aid to the Elderly—were shifted into the Social Security Administration and renamed SSI.

As of 2013, both SSDI and SSI operated with similar definitions of disability. Under both programs, applicants must be severely disabled, meaning they have a long-term or permanent physical or mental condition that prevents them from doing any type of substantial gainful activity or work. The Social Security Administration uses its own medical experts to evaluate disability claims and bases its decisions on a list of physical and mental conditions contained in its regulations. In addition, to meet eligibility criteria, disability applicants must show that they have worked a minimum period of time during the ten years prior to the onset of disability. After their disability claim is granted, disabled persons received a monthly cash payment, typically between $500 and $2,000. After twenty-four months of receiving SSDI benefits, disabled persons become eligible for Medicare benefits. Once disabled beneficiaries reach retirement age, they can also apply for Social Security retirement benefits. Similarly, the spouse or children of SSDI beneficiaries may be eligible for Social Security benefits.

Of the two programs only SSI is based on financial need. For SSI, applicants must be disabled, blind, or age sixty-five or older, with no or low income. The income limits are set by each state, but typically they range from $500 to $700 per month. SSI applicants may not have countable resources worth more than $2,000 ($3,000 for a married couple). If the SSI application is approved, the applicant receives a monthly cash payment of at least $674 ($1,101 for couples), although some states add to this amount. In addition, the SSI beneficiary becomes eligible for Medicaid, food stamps, rehabilitation, and home care, if needed.

The Social Security disability program, according to a 2012 trustees report, has been spending more than it receives in taxes for several years and is expected to run out of trust fund money in 2016, much faster than the retirement portion of the Social Security program. The authors of the viewpoints in this chapter debate the basic question of Social Security's solvency and whether it is going bankrupt.

Social Security Is Going Broke

Paul Ryan

Paul Ryan is a US Republican congressman from Wisconsin; the chairman of the House Budget Committee; and part of the Tea Party, a group of conservative Republicans that promotes spending cuts and opposes tax increases. Ryan was the Republican candidate for vice president in 2012.

Social Security provides vital financial support for more than 54 million seniors. Social Security also provides critical benefits to widows and those with disabilities. Unfortunately, Social Security faces a $6.5 trillion deficit over the next 75 years (an amount equal to over one-third the size of the entire U.S. economy). With 10,000 "Baby Boomers" turning 65 every day, it is essential that we work to preserve the programs these seniors have come to count on. As Chairman House Budget Committee, one of my top priorities is to preserve the Social Security safety net and make sure the program remains solvent for future generations.

Social Security Is Going Broke

Social Security is funded by the payroll taxes of current workers to pay the benefits of current retirees. Projected long run program costs are not sustainable under current program parameters. The Social Security Trustees project that the cash flow deficits that began in 2010 will continue permanently. That means that to pay full Social Security benefits, the government must cut spending, raise taxes, or borrow more money to finance pension payments.

A central factor in the looming financial crunch is the fact that our society is aging. The "Baby Boom" generation has already started to collect their Social Security retirement ben-

Paul Ryan, "Social Security," paulryan.house.gov, n.d.

efits. As a result, there are fewer workers to support each retiree than when Social Security was created. Increasing life expectancy and the approaching retirement of more Baby Boomers continues to put increasing pressure on Social Security each year. Over the next several years, the number of retirees is expected to grow more rapidly than the number of individuals whose taxes will pay for future benefits. Because of this, the number of workers supporting each Social Security recipient is projected to fall from 3.3 today to 2.2 in 2041. When comparing these figures with those from 1950 (when there were 16 workers for every 1 recipient), the challenges of the program become clear.

Any value in the balances in the Social Security trust fund is derived from dubious government accounting.

The Need for Reform

According to the 2011 Social Security Trustees Report, beneficiaries will face a painful 23 percent benefit cut in 2036 when the Social Security Trust fund is exhausted. These reductions are expected to grow to 26 percent in 2085. Even those who are currently on Social Security—those now 62 and older— may experience indiscriminate cuts in benefits at a time when they are increasingly reliant on the program.

The Path to Prosperity

A common reaction to the question of what to do about the problem with Social Security has unfortunately been, "What problem?" The deniers claim that the Social Security trust fund will remain solvent for another 16 years, at which point the government could theoretically cover the shortfall by raising taxes. Others downplay whether any changes to Social Security will be necessary—they claim that sustained economic growth could take care of the problem all by itself.

Neither is correct. First, any value in the balances in the Social Security trust fund is derived from dubious government accounting. The trust fund is not a real savings account. From 1983 to 2011, the trust fund collected more in Social Security taxes than it paid out in Social Security benefits. But the government borrowed all of these surpluses and spent them on other government programs unrelated to Social Security. The trust fund holds Treasury securities, but the ability to redeem these securities is completely dependent on the Treasury's ability to raise money through taxes or borrowing.

Beginning in 2010, Social Security started paying out more in benefits than it collected in taxes—a trend that will skyrocket as the baby boomers continue to retire. In order to pay full benefits, the government must pay back the money it owes Social Security.

Those who wish to solve this problem by raising taxes are ignoring the profound economic damage that such a large tax increases would entail. Just lifting the cap on income subject to Social Security taxes, as some have proposed, would, when combined with the [Barack] Obama administration's other preferred tax policies, lift the top marginal tax rate to over 60 percent. In reality, lifting the cap on income subject to Social Security will hurt the self employed—like many of the farmers and small business men and women in the First District—hardest as these individuals pay both the employee and employer share of the Social Security tax and further hamper the economic growth these individuals can provide.

Most economists agree that raising marginal tax rates that high would create a significant drag on economic growth, job creation, productivity and wages. This nation cannot fix its retirement-security system by leaving young families with nothing to save.

President [Franklin D.] Roosevelt himself viewed Social Security as an evolving program. As he wrote in a 1939 message to Congress, "We shall make the most orderly progress if we look upon Social Security as a development toward a goal rather than a finished product. We shall make the most lasting progress if we recognize that Social Security can furnish only a base upon which each one of our citizens may build his individual security through his own individual efforts."

The evolution must continue today, because Social Security's fragile condition poses a serious problem that threatens to break the broader compact in which workers support the generation preceding them, and earn the support of those who follow.

I believe there is a bipartisan path forward on Social Security—one that requires all parties first to acknowledge the fiscal realities of this critical program. The President's Fiscal Commission made a positive first step by advancing solutions to ensure the solvency of Social Security.

While certain details of the Commission's Social Security proposals, particularly on the tax side, are of debatable merit, the Commission undoubtedly made positive steps forward on bipartisan solutions to strengthen Social Security. The House-passed budget builds upon the Commission's work, forcing action to solve this pressing problem by requiring the President to put forward specific ideas on fixing Social Security.

In a shared call for leadership, the budget also puts the onus on Congress to offer legislation to ensure the sustainable solvency of this critical program. Both parties must work together to chart a path forward on common sense reforms, and the House-passed budget provides the nation's leaders with the tools to get there.

The Social Security Trust Fund Will Be Exhausted in 2033

The Board of Trustees, Federal Old-Age and Survivors Insurance and Federal Disability Insurance Trust Funds

The Board of Trustees, Federal Old-Age and Survivors Insurance and Federal Disability Insurance Trust Funds oversees and issues annual reports on the financial health of the federal Social Security program.

The Old-Age, Survivors, and Disability Insurance (OASDI) program makes monthly income available to insured workers and their families at retirement, death, or disability. The OASDI program consists of two parts. Retired workers, their families, and survivors of deceased workers receive monthly benefits under the Old-Age and Survivors Insurance (OASI) program. Disabled workers and their families receive monthly benefits under the Disability Insurance (DI) program.

The Social Security Act established the Board of Trustees to oversee the financial operations of the OASI and DI Trust Funds. The Board is composed of six members. Four members serve by virtue of their positions in the Federal Government: the Secretary of the Treasury, who is the Managing Trustee; the Secretary of Labor; the Secretary of Health and Human Services; and the Commissioner of Social Security. The President appoints and the Senate confirms the other two members to serve as public representatives. The Deputy Commissioner of the Social Security Administration (SSA) serves as Secretary of the Board.

The Board of Trustees, Federal Old-Age and Survivors Insurance and Federal Disability Insurance Trust Funds, "The 2012 Annual Report of the Board of Trustees of the Federal Old-Age and Survivors Insurance and Federal Disability Insurance Trust Funds," April 25, 2012, pp. 1–5.

The Social Security Act requires that the Board, among other duties, report annually to the Congress on the actuarial status and financial operations of the OASI and DI Trust Funds. The 2012 report is the 72nd such report. . . .

In 2011

At the end of 2011, the OASDI program was providing benefits to about 55 million people: 38 million retired workers and dependents of retired workers, 6 million survivors of deceased workers, and 11 million disabled workers and dependents of disabled workers. During the year, an estimated 158 million people had earnings covered by Social Security and paid payroll taxes. Total expenditures in 2011 were $736 billion. Total income was $805 billion, which consisted of $691 billion in non-interest income and $114 billion in interest earnings. Assets held in special issue U.S. Treasury securities grew to $2.7 trillion.

Short-Range Results

In 2011, Social Security's cost continued to exceed both the program's tax income and its non-interest income, a trend that the Trustees project to continue throughout the short-range period and beyond. The 2011 deficit of tax income relative to cost was $148 billion, and the projected 2012 deficit is $165 billion. The sizes of these deficits are largely due to a temporary reduction in the Social Security payroll tax for 2011 and 2012. The legislation establishing the payroll tax reduction also provided for transfers from the General Fund of the Treasury to the trust funds to "replicate to the extent possible" revenues that would have occurred in the absence of the payroll tax reduction. Including these general revenue reimbursements, the 2011 deficit of non-interest income relative to cost was $45 billion, and the projected 2012 deficit is $53 billion.

The Trustees project that the assets of the OASI Trust Fund and of the combined OASI and DI Trust Funds will be adequate over the next 10 years under the intermediate assumptions. However, the projected assets of the DI Trust Fund decline steadily, fall below 100 percent of annual cost by the beginning of 2013, and continue to decline until the trust fund is exhausted in 2016. The DI Trust Fund does not satisfy the short-range test of financial adequacy because the test requires that the trust fund remain above 100 percent of annual cost throughout the short-range period.

The dollar level of the combined trust funds declines beginning in 2021 until assets are exhausted in 2033.

The Trustees project that the combined assets of the OASI and DI Trust Funds will increase for the next several years, growing from $2,678 billion at the beginning of 2012 to $3,061 billion at the beginning of 2021. At the same time, the ratio of assets to cost continues to decline, from 340 percent of annual cost for 2012 to 227 percent of annual cost for 2021. Assets increase because annual cost is less than total income for 2012 through 2020. Beginning in 2021, however, annual cost exceeds total income, and therefore assets begin to decline, reaching $3,053 billion at the beginning of 2022. Excluding interest earned on trust fund assets from the comparison, annual cost exceeds non-interest income in 2012 and remains higher throughout the remainder of the short-range period. For last year's report, the Trustees projected that combined assets would be 347 percent of annual cost at the beginning of 2012 and 272 percent at the beginning of 2021. Projected trust fund assets decline more quickly than in last year's report principally due to updated economic data and assumptions.

Long-Range Results

The Trustees project that annual cost will exceed non-interest income throughout the long-range period under the intermediate assumptions. The dollar level of the combined trust funds declines beginning in 2021 until assets are exhausted in 2033. Considered separately, the DI Trust Fund becomes exhausted in 2016 and the OASI Trust Fund becomes exhausted in 2035. The projected exhaustion date occurs two years earlier for the DI Trust Fund and three years earlier for the OASI Trust Fund and the combined OASI and DI Trust Funds.

The projected OASDI annual cost rate increases from 13.83 percent of taxable payroll for 2012 to 17.41 percent for 2035.

Projected OASDI cost generally increases more rapidly than projected non-interest income through 2035 because the retirement of the baby-boom generation will increase the number of beneficiaries much faster than subsequent lower-birth-rate generations increase the number of workers. From 2035 to 2050, the cost rate declines due principally to the aging of the already retired baby-boom generation. Thereafter, increases in life expectancy cause OASDI cost to increase generally relative to non-interest income, but more slowly than prior to 2035.

The projected OASDI annual cost rate increases from 13.83 percent of taxable payroll for 2012 to 17.41 percent for 2035 and to 17.83 percent for 2086, a level that is 4.50 percent of taxable payroll more than the projected income rate for 2086. For last year's report, the Trustees estimated the OASDI cost for 2086 at 17.59 percent, or 4.28 percent of payroll more than the annual income rate for that year. Expressed in relation to the projected gross domestic product (GDP) [a measure of the nation's total economic output], OASDI cost rises from the current level of 5.0 percent of GDP to about 6.4 percent by 2035, then declines to 6.1 percent by 2055, and remains between 6.0 and 6.1 percent through 2086.

For the 75-year projection period, the actuarial deficit is 2.67 percent of taxable payroll, 0.44 percentage point larger than in last year's report. The open group unfunded obligation for OASDI over the 75-year period is $8.6 trillion in present value and is $2.1 trillion more than the measured level of a year ago. If the assumptions, methods, starting values, and the law had all remained unchanged, the unfunded obligation would have risen to about $7.0 trillion due to the change in the valuation date. The remaining increase in the unfunded obligation is primarily due to updated data and economic assumptions.

Lawmakers would have to make significantly larger changes for future beneficiaries if they decide to avoid changes for current beneficiaries and those close to retirement age.

Legislative Action Is Needed

Under the long-range intermediate assumptions, the Trustees project that annual cost for the OASDI program will exceed non-interest income in 2012 and remain higher throughout the remainder of the long-range period. The projected combined OASI and DI Trust Fund assets increase through 2020, begin to decline in 2021, and become exhausted and unable to pay scheduled benefits in full on a timely basis in 2033. However, the DI Trust Fund becomes exhausted in 2016, so legislative action is needed as soon as possible. In the absence of a long-term solution, lawmakers could reallocate the payroll tax rate between OASI and DI, as they did in 1994.

For the combined OASI and DI Trust Funds to remain solvent throughout the 75-year projection period, lawmakers could: (1) increase the combined payroll tax rate for the period in a manner equivalent to an immediate and permanent increase of 2.61 percentage points (from its current level of

12.40 percent to 15.01 percent); (2) reduce scheduled benefits for the period in a manner equivalent to an immediate and permanent reduction of 16.2 percent; (3) draw on alternative sources of revenue; or (4) adopt some combination of these approaches. Lawmakers would have to make significantly larger changes for future beneficiaries if they decide to avoid changes for current beneficiaries and those close to retirement age.

The Trustees recommend that lawmakers address the projected trust fund shortfalls in a timely way in order to phase in necessary changes and give workers and beneficiaries time to adjust to them. Implementing changes soon would allow more generations to share in the needed revenue increases or reductions in scheduled benefits. Social Security will play a critical role in the lives of 56 million beneficiaries and 159 million covered workers and their families in 2012. With informed discussion, creative thinking, and timely legislative action, Social Security can continue to protect future generations.

Social Security Goes Bankrupt

John Hayward

John Hayward is an author and a staff writer for Human Events, *a conservative newspaper.*

According to new projections from the Congressional Budget Office [a federal agency that provides fiscal advice to Congress], Social Security will officially go bankrupt this year [2011], paying out $45 billion more in benefits than it takes in. Until now, Social Security defenders have briskly assured us this would not happen for twenty or thirty years, but those who ignored the political spin and looked at the actual numbers knew it was coming much sooner.

This is an important milestone in the utter collapse of American socialism. The cold reality of Social Security insolvency hopelessly discredits the premise of government-assured prosperity for all, financed by "contributions" from taxpayers and businesses. No aspect of liberal economic philosophy can survive in the minds of those who understand the impact of this news.

Social Security has always been part of the Big Lie repeated in President [Barack] Obama's State of the Union address. Wise politicians do not have vast resources available to "win the future" by over-riding competition with political judgment. They can't create successful industries through vast subsidies. They've *never had that kind of money.*

American socialists have been raiding the Social Security "trust fund" for decades, to make the rest of the government look less insolvent than it really is. The funds are stuffed with IOUs, which count as "assets" for Social Security . . . but are not counted as liabilities for the general Treasury fund.

This year, we reach the point where Social Security must pay substantially more in benefits than it takes in, and there's no "cash reserve" to tap into, no "lockbox" full of money that can fund the program for a while longer. The excess is coming right out of general revenue. This is the year when Social Security transforms from a secret piggy bank that lets Big Government pretend it has lots of money to spend, into another massive expense it must cover.

Modern liberals are trying to float the idea of raising the employer contributions to Social Security this time, without increasing employee deductions.

One of the liberal canards that dies with Social Security bankruptcy is the notion we can "tax our way out of deficits." We tried that a couple of times before with this particular Big Government albatross. [Former president] Jimmy Carter tripled the FICA [Federal Insurance Contributions Act tax, which funds Social Security] tax rates in 1977, and promised it would make Social Security solvent until 2030. Wrong. Dead wrong.

Modern liberals are trying to float the idea of raising the employer contributions to Social Security this time, without increasing employee deductions—in other words, another hidden tax, added to the pile of glass bricks already carried by a private sector wrestling with double-digit unemployment. Just because you don't see those taxes on your paycheck stub doesn't mean they are not real. Employers would pass those extra costs along to employees and consumers, through reduced wages and increased prices . . . or they'd just cut back on the amount of increasingly expensive labor they purchase.

Social Security is the eternal proof that if you raise taxes to repair a deficit, *liberals will just spend the money.* That's what happened to Jimmy Carter's massive FICA hike. That money didn't go into some kind of safety-deposit box. The government spent it to finance other programs, and here we are, bankrupt in 2010 instead of 2030.

This is why Social Security *must* be privatized. Would you willingly invest in a private fund which subsidized all the stupid, wasteful, and morally abhorrent things Big Government has been spending your Social Security "contributions" on? A fund manager who gave the kind of speech Barack Obama delivered in the State of the Union would have been laughed out of the room before the speech was over. Solar shingles? High-speed rail? More billions for a failed education bureaucracy? He would have been crushed beneath the stampede of fleeing stockholders.

Look at it this way: Social Security is not *and never was—* investment made by the young, to be collected when they grow old. It's a system of current workers paying the benefits for current retirees—a Ponzi scheme. The ratio of workers to retirees has been falling rapidly. The *last* thing we can afford to do is accelerate that process by reducing the number of workers . . . and that's exactly what tax increases do.

There is nothing politicians love to do more than buy political support with future commitments, which someone else will have to pay for. Taking back such a promise produces howls of outrage from its dependen[ts] who are grimly determine[d] to collect what they are owed. That's why union pension plans are out of control, and that's why Social Security is falling apart. Politicians will make all the unsustainable commitments we let them get away with. Social Security and Medicare, the worst ones they ever made, are melting down before our eyes . . . after a century of generating revenue that allowed government to grow larger in a thousand other ways.

Social Security Is Not Going Broke

David Cay Johnston

David Cay Johnston is a journalist and the author of several bestselling books, including Free Lunch: How the Wealthiest Americans Enrich Themselves at Government Expense (and Stick You with the Bill), *published in 2009.*

Which federal program took in more than it spent last year, added $95 billion to its surplus and lifted 20 million Americans of all ages out of poverty?

Why, Social Security, of course, which ended 2011 with a $2.7 trillion surplus.

That surplus is almost twice the $1.4 trillion collected in personal and corporate income taxes last year. And it is projected to go on growing until 2021, the year the youngest Baby Boomers turn 67 and qualify for full old-age benefits.

So why all the talk about Social Security "going broke"? That theme filled the news after release of the latest annual report of the Federal Old-Age and Survivors Insurance and Federal Disability Insurance Trust Funds, as Social Security is formally called.

The reason is that the people who want to kill Social Security have for years worked hard to persuade the young that the Social Security taxes they pay to support today's gray hairs will do nothing for them when their own hair turns gray.

That narrative has become the conventional wisdom because it is easily reduced to a headline or sound bite. The facts, which require more nuance and detail, show that, with a few fixes, Social Security can be safe for as long as we want.

Shifting Tax Burdens

Let's look at how Social Security taxes have grown in the last half century—a little-known tale of tax burdens shifted off the rich and onto workers. From 1961 through 2011, the year covered in the last Social Security report, Social Security taxes exploded from 3.1 percent of Gross Domestic Product to 5.5 percent.

[Because] the Social Security tax is capped, most of the burden of the increased-payroll tax went to the bottom 90 percent.

Income taxes went the other way. The personal income tax slipped from 7.8 percent of the economy to 7.3 percent, with most of the decline enjoyed by people in the top 1 percent of incomes. The big drop was in the corporate income tax, which fell from 4 percent of the economy to 1.2 percent. Notice that the corporate income tax fell by 2.8 percentage points, an amount almost entirely offset by a 2.4 percentage point increase in Social Security taxes.

The effect has been to ease the taxes of the wealthy, while burdening the vast majority of workers. Considering how highly ownership of stocks is concentrated, the benefit of those lower corporate taxes went overwhelmingly to the top 1 percent and, especially, the top 1 percent of the top 1 percent. Considering that the Social Security tax is capped, most of the burden of the increased-payroll tax went to the bottom 90 percent.

Now let's look at how that $2.7 trillion Social Security surplus arose. In 1983, President Ronald Reagan sponsored an increase in Social Security taxes, changing the program from pay-as-you-go to collecting much more taxes than it paid in benefits. The idea was to have the Boomers prepay part of their old age benefits. The extra tax was supposed to pay off the federal debt and then be invested in federal bonds. Instead, Reagan ran huge deficits, violating his 1980 promise to balance the federal budget within three years of taking office.

Financing Tax Cuts

In my view, building the Social Security surplus has had two major effects.

One effect was to finance tax cuts for those at the top, whose highest tax rate fell during the Reagan years from 70 percent to 28 percent, and for corporations, whose rate fell from 50 percent of profits to 35 percent. Those with less subsidized those with more.

The other effect was a huge increase in consumer debt, as Americans saddled with higher Social Security taxes took out loans to cover other needs. Stagnant wages played a role, but the $2.7 trillion Social Security surplus is also a factor in a $1.5 trillion increase in consumer debt since 1984.

It is no wonder consumers have gone into debt. Paying a tax in advance is expensive. Indeed, the first lesson in tax planning is that a tax deferred for 30 years is effectively a tax avoided, provided the money is invested wisely. The reverse is also true. A dollar of tax paid in 1984 cost $2.20 in today's dollars, and that's before counting the interest that could have been earned.

With the coming bulge in retirees, Social Security will start to pay out more than it takes in 2021, according to projections in the latest annual report. Under current law the program would be able to pay only about three-quarters of promised benefits starting in 2033. But that scenario can easily be avoided through a combination of four policy changes that would ensure full benefits continue to be paid, though I fear Congress will continue to do nothing.

One would be restoring the Reagan standard that 90 percent of wages are covered by the Social Security tax, which now applies to only 83 percent of wages. If we went back to the Reagan standard, the Social Security tax would apply to close to $200,000 of wages this year instead of $110,100.

Two would be raising the Social Security tax rate by two percentage points. That tax hike could be smaller or even avoided if, three, we reignited the growth in wages. Median wages have fallen in 2010 back to the level of 1999. And, four, it would help just as much if we created millions more jobs, which since 2000 have grown at only a fifth the rate of population increases.

Under current tax rules, the Social Security shortfall for the next 75 years is $8.6 trillion.

But there is a much bigger problem that needs our attention. If we continue national security spending at current levels, with no future increases, the total cost would be $63 trillion, based on the figures in President Barack Obama's latest budget. Unlike spending on Social Security, much of the national security spending goes overseas. And that makes us worse off.

Social Security Does Not Have Serious Financial Problems

Jane Bryant Quinn

Jane Bryant Quinn is a personal finance expert, an author, and a regular contributor to the AARP Bulletin, *a monthly magazine and website with information for Americans who are fifty and older.*

It happened during the stock boom of the 1990s, and it is happening again. Social Security is coming under attack. The first challenge arose from hope—that savers would get more retirement income for their money if they bought stocks. But the idea of privatization was not popular with the public.

Now, the attack comes from fear—that Social Security has serious financial problems and can only fail. Younger people lean more toward change than older people do. A CNN/Opinion Research Corp. poll conducted a year ago [2010] found that 60 percent of adults who aren't retired expect to get nothing—zero—from Social Security in their older age.

They're mistaken. As misinformation and mistrust grow, however, it becomes important to explore—and explode—several Social Security myths that endanger the system's public support.

Exploding the Myths

Myth No. 1: Social Security is going bankrupt. No, it's not. Even in the unlikely event that nothing changes and the program's entire surplus runs out in 2036, as projected, checks would keep coming. Payroll taxes at current rates would cover

77 percent of all the future benefits promised. That's true for young and old alike, and includes inflation adjustments.

Myth No. 2: I'd be better off if I'd kept my Social Security taxes in my own investment account. Hmmm—you're saying that you'd faithfully put that money aside, every year of your working life, in a mix of stocks and bonds, without ever skipping a year, drawing on your nest egg or selling when the market dropped? Few such paragons exist.

In 1983, Congress made changes to Social Security to build a fund that would pay for boomers when they retire.

You'd need to invest far more than you probably realize to match the benefits Social Security pays. As an example, take a 65-year-old couple with a single breadwinner who earned the average wage. At retirement, they'd currently get about $2,170 a month, plus inflation adjustments, for life, the Urban Institute reports.

To equal that sum in private savings, they'd need to have about $580,000, says Michael Kitces, director of research for Pinnacle Advisory Group, and the money might last only 30 years. How many average earners are likely to save that much?

Myth No. 3: In 1983, Congress made changes to Social Security to build a fund that would pay for boomers when they retire, so it's not fair to change benefits now. No, Congress did not intend to "advance fund" the boomers, according to a study of the record by Charles Blahous of Stanford University's Hoover Institution. It raised taxes and cut some future benefits to cure an imminent insolvency. The trust fund reserves—now $2.6 trillion—were a by-product of the decisions made. Congress never veered from its vision of intergenerational compact: Working people pay for those who don't, or can't, work anymore. On the flip side, the compact requires older people to make some concessions so that younger people can afford it.

Myth No. 4: You should get out of Social Security the amount you put in. No. Social Security is not an individual investment program. Your taxes paid for the earlier generation of retirees. Current workers are paying for you. The total amount of your benefit depends on how much you earned, whether you get a spousal benefit, when you retire and how long you live.

Myth No. 5: Social Security helps old people, not younger people like me. Wrong. It provides income support to qualified widows and widowers with young children, as well as orphans. Just as important, it saves young families from the cost of supporting older parents who, without Social Security, wouldn't have enough money to live on. It also provides benefits for workers who become disabled.

My final point . . . and it isn't a myth, it's a fact. If young people switched their payroll taxes into private accounts, the government would have to borrow $6.5 trillion or more (depending on the details) to keep paying out benefits to current retirees.

That means higher deficits, higher income taxes, further slashes in spending, or all three. It's smarter—and cheaper—to fix the current program and put everyone's mind at rest.

It Is Impossible for Social Security to Go Bankrupt

John T. Harvey

John T. Harvey is a professor of economics at Texas Christian University, in Forth Worth, Texas; he is also a contributor to Forbes, *a business and financial news magazine.*

It is a logical impossibility for Social Security to go bankrupt. We can voluntarily choose to suspend or eliminate the program, but it could never fail because it "ran out of money." This belief is the result of a common error: conceptualizing Social Security from the micro (individual) rather than the macro (economy-wide) perspective. It's not a pension fund into which you put your money when you are young and from which you draw when you are old. It's an immediate transfer from workers today to retirees today. That's what it has always been and that's what it has to be—there is no other possible way for it to work.

To explain this, let's create a simple world. Say there has been some sort of terrible global calamity and we only have ten people left. Further say that these ten decide to make the best of it and set up a society, including an economy. Of course, much of humanity's technology is now lost to us, so our level of productivity is very low. As a starting point, assume that each of us is only able to produce enough output for herself or himself to survive.

How many people can retire under these circumstances? Obviously, none. Anyone who stops working, starves. It is irrelevant how many people over 65, disabled, or otherwise deserving there are, no one can quit because our level of productivity is too low. Nor is it helpful to have a pile of cash somewhere. No amount of money can change the fact that one person can only make enough goods and services for one person. If there are ten people to feed, clothe, and shelter, then ten people must work. This reality is inescapable and is the reason why the real determinant of the feasibility of Social Security (or any other type of retirement system, private or public) is productivity. If it falls short, then supporting a class of retirees is impossible, regardless of how much cash we have on hand; if it does not, however, financing it is trivial. This will be shown below.

We . . . need to agree on how many people get to retire, what the criteria are, and what their share will be.

Now let's say it's been several years and we have been able to increase our productivity. To make the math simple, double it. This gives us some options:

1. We could all keep working and just double our standard of living.

2. Five people could keep working and share half of their stuff with the other five, giving us each the same standard of living as at the start.

3. We could adopt an intermediate position with more than zero but fewer than five retirees, allowing us both a chance to retire and a higher standard of living.

The third would probably be the most attractive, and it is what we have actually experienced. Productivity growth has been such that, not only have people been able to retire, but we are each better off, too. Assuming we follow this path, what is the next step?

First, we would need to agree on how many people get to retire, what the criteria are, and what their share will be. As that's more politics than economics, however, I won't say too much about it other than to say that there is no reason to assume that the retirees should get exactly the same cut as the workers. We could decide they get more, less, or the same. The possibilities are determined by productivity, while the specifics are a function of our sense of justice and our national philosophy (and, if we are realistic about it, the distribution of power).

Maintaining a class of retirees (whether via Social Security or private pensions) means redistributing existing output, not putting money under your mattress.

To make the example concrete, say we decided that three of our survivors qualify for retirement (leaving seven workers) and that we will all get equal shares. This would mean that each worker would get to keep 70% of what they produced, passing the remaining 30% to the retirees (if you grab a calculator, you'll see that gives everyone the same share—however, understanding this is not important to the rest of the story). And that's it—we are done. With only ten people, it doesn't need to get any more complicated. We have a retirement system and we don't need to talk about money at all. We just say stuff like, "Hey, Bob! I caught ten fish today—which three do you want?"

In the real world, however, there are more than ten people and thus the coordination of this effort becomes much more complex. And this is where money comes in. Its function is to enable the transfer of output from current workers to current retirees in a world where we are not all neighbors. Money does not, to reiterate, have anything whatsoever to do with whether or not we can support retirees, how many they can be, or how much they can have. That is 100% a result of productivity. Money is only the mechanism we use to make sure Bob gets his three fish.

To give it a more realistic feel, change the numbers from 7 workers and 3 retirees to 70 million and 30 million. Now what to do? Even if we have unanimous agreement on our plan, how can we make sure that retirees get their cut if it is no longer as easy as picking three fish from a basket full of ten? The most obvious and straightforward means is this: set a tax of 30% on the salaries of existing workers and give it directly to the retirees—right now, today, immediately. Have the money come straight out of your paycheck and right into your grandmother's bank account. This accomplishes the goal neatly and directly—and it's exactly what we do in real life. This is how Social Security actually operates. As you can see, this needs no prior financing or savings, nor would that appear to be particularly helpful. At the national level, maintaining a class of retirees (whether via Social Security or private pensions) means redistributing existing output, not putting money under your mattress. Although *you* can run out of money for retirement, we, as a nation, cannot.

The trust fund is worth having as a buffer, but it has zero to do with the feasibility of the system. If it runs out tomorrow, we can still have Social Security.

What, then, you may ask, is the Social Security Trust Fund, the pool of money that people say will dry up and make it impossible for anyone to receive their Social Security payments? It is the surplus that resulted from having collected more in taxes than was necessary to pay out to retirees. Let me say that again: it is how much existing workers were overtaxed relative to the need to pay retirees in the past. It was never the source of the money we've been paying to Social Security recipients all these years. Strictly speaking, it's completely unnecessary if we are able to precisely and continuously match tax revenues and pay outs.

We cannot do that, of course, partly because we are dealing with millions of people in a complex economy. In addition, while the payments to retirees are fairly formulaic and change in a predictable way (we can figure how many people are about to reach eligibility and how much they will draw), the revenues fluctuate with the state of the economy. They rise during expansions and fall during recessions. The trust fund can therefore serve as a place to park excess revenues when taxes exceed expenditures and from which additional funds can be drawn when the reverse occurs. It's a buffer, sort of like that give-a-penny-take-a-penny tray at the local convenience store. As always, however, productivity and productivity alone determines our ability to support a class of retirees. This is only about how we coordinate that system.

There is another trust fund issue and it is the one related to the expected increase in the ratio of retirees to workers over the next couple of decades. This would presumably cause a net drain on the fund since payments to retirees might increase relative to tax revenues. This is actually the specific phenomenon to which many people are referring when they say that Social Security is going to go bankrupt. However, a) there is no guarantee this will occur since rising productivity could drive up wages sufficiently to compensate (although our trend of stagnating wages relative to profits is frustrating this) and b) even if that did occur, this hardly means that Social Security is kaput. Any shortfall can always be addressed in a very straightforward and supremely logical fashion: raise taxes or lower benefits (and it is exceedingly likely that even if this occurs, we aren't talking about anything drastic). It bears emphasizing, however, that such changes would still be a function of productivity and have absolutely, positively nothing to do with how much money we have or haven't saved up. Funding, finances, money, taxes, etc. are part of the coordination mechanism, not the feasibility.

The lesson from this is that if we want Social Security to "be there" when we retire, our efforts must be focused on increasing productivity and making sure in particular that these increases get passed on to workers in the form of higher wages. But raising the value of the trust fund is, in this respect, pointless. Even if we had an infinite amount of money in it such that we could reduce all workers' taxes to zero and still pay retirees, the exact same thing is still happening: Bob is getting three fish from the basket of ten, leaving seven for the original fisherman. Whether we accomplish this via direct taxation or from a pool of funds is absolutely, totally irrelevant in terms of the underlying economic impact (except for the fact that paying retirees from a fund is likely to cause inflation—explaining why is a little complicated so I don't pursue it here). We are fooling ourselves if we think that taking money from the trust fund is giving us a free lunch. If there are only ten fish, there are only ten fish. Nothing other than changing productivity can affect that. The trust fund is worth having as a buffer, but it has zero to do with the feasibility of the system. If it runs out tomorrow, we can still have Social Security because we still have ten fish.

Incidentally, there appears to be every indication that productivity increases should be sufficient for the Baby Boomers to retire AND allow the rest of us to enjoy even higher standards of living (assuming the compression of wages ends). That's good news. In fact, it's the only news that's important.

In closing, I'm not telling you whether you should be for or against Social Security, but the argument that it is going bankrupt is a non-starter. It is much ado about nothing.

CHAPTER 2

Is Social Security a Successful Government Program?

Chapter Preface

Social Security provides an important source of retirement and disability income for women. Women can qualify for Social Security benefits in a number of ways. Like working men, women who work pay taxes into the Social Security system and are equally able to qualify for and receive benefits based on their work record. In addition, under Social Security rules, women who do not work or who work sporadically throughout their lives can qualify for spousal benefits based on their husband's earnings when their husband retires, becomes disabled, or dies. Divorced women are also protected and awarded Social Security spousal benefits (and benefits for children) if the marriage lasted at least ten years and other conditions are met.

Social Security is vital for women because they are more likely to earn less than men over their lifetime. According to the Social Security Administration, the median earnings of women who worked full-time, year-round in 2011 were $36,500, compared to $48,000 for men. In addition, many women take time out from work to care for children, spouses, and parents. Given that Social Security retirement benefits are based on earnings, these women often receive lower benefit amounts than men who do not take time off. In 2011, for example, the government estimates that the average annual Social Security income received by women sixty-five years and older was $12,188, compared to $15,795 for men. However, the Social Security system's progressive design provides some help to women because lower-wage earners receive higher percentages in Social Security benefits than high-earning persons.

Women also typically are less likely than men to have other retirement income or assets, and thus they are more dependent on Social Security benefits during their later years. Although working women in 2013 were participating more in employer-sponsored retirement plans than in the past, older women were less likely than older men to have significant pension income other than Social Security. Unmarried women fare worse than married women, who often benefit from their husbands' pension income and assets. As of 2010, the government estimates only 22.6 percent of unmarried women aged sixty-five or older were receiving private pension income, compared to 27.3 percent of unmarried men. As a result, Social Security comprises a larger portion of retirement income for women than for men. The Social Security Administration estimates that for unmarried and widowed women age sixty-five and older in 2011, Social Security made up 50 percent of their total income, whereas Social Security benefits comprised only 36 percent of unmarried and widowed men's total income. In fact, almost half of all elderly unmarried women relied on Social Security for 90 percent or more of their income in 2011. In addition, women live on average about five years longer than men and have a greater chance of exhausting their assets; therefore, they often rely on Social Security for a longer period than men.

Recent statistics show that women are the majority in the pool of people receiving Social Security benefits—approximately 60 percent of that pool, according to government sources. This Social Security income is often the difference between having enough and abject poverty for women. In 2011, according to the National Women's Law Center, Social Security benefits helped keep 11.7 million women out of poverty, including 8.7 million women age sixty-five and older, and more than 3 million younger women age eighteen to sixty-four, along with almost 1.1 million children. Without Social Security, poverty rates for women would be much higher, especially for older and minority women, who disproportionately depend more on Social Security. Indeed, even with Social Security, more than twice as many elderly women as men lived in poverty in 2011. Poverty rates are highest for African

American and Hispanic women aged sixty-five and older. The authors of the viewpoints in this chapter note the anti-poverty value of Social Security and offer their views on the overall effectiveness of the Social Security program.

Social Security Is One of the Most Successful US Domestic Programs

Center on Budget and Policy Priorities

The Center on Budget and Policy Priorities is an organization that works on fiscal policy and public programs affecting low- and moderate-income Americans and develops proposals for fighting poverty.

President Franklin Roosevelt signed the Social Security Act on August 14, 1935. As Social Security celebrates its 75th anniversary, it remains one of the nation's most successful, effective, and popular programs. It provides a foundation of income on which workers can build to plan for their retirement. It also provides valuable social insurance protection to workers who become disabled and to families whose breadwinner dies.

Fact #1: Social Security is more than just a retirement program. It provides important life insurance and disability insurance protection as well.

In June 2010, 53.4 million people, or about one in every six U.S. residents, collected Social Security benefits. While three-quarters of them received benefits as retirees or elderly widow(er)s, another 10.0 million (19 percent) received disability insurance benefits, and 2.3 million (4 percent) received benefits as young survivors of deceased workers.

Workers earn life insurance and disability insurance protection by making Social Security payroll tax contributions:

About 97 percent of people aged 20–49 who worked in covered employment in 2009 have earned life insurance pro-

Center on Budget and Policy Priorities, "Policy Basics: Top Ten Facts about Social Security on the Program's 75th Anniversary," August 13, 2010. Copyright © 2010 by Center on Budget and Policy Priorities. All rights reserved. Reproduced by permission.

tection through Social Security. For a young worker with average earnings, a spouse, and two children, that Social Security protection is equivalent to a life insurance policy with a face value of $433,000.

Social Security provides a guaranteed, progressive benefit that keeps up with increases in the cost of living.

About 91 percent of people aged 21–64 who worked in covered employment in 2009 are insured through Social Security in case of disability.

The risk of disability or premature death is greater than many people realize. Almost four in ten men (38 percent) recently entering the labor force and three in ten women (31 percent) will become disabled or die before reaching the full retirement age.

Fact #2: Social Security provides a guaranteed, progressive benefit that keeps up with increases in the cost of living.

Social Security benefits are based on the earnings on which you pay Social Security payroll taxes. The higher are your earnings (up to a maximum taxable amount, currently $106,800), the higher will be your benefit.

Social Security benefits are progressive: they represent a higher proportion of a worker's previous earnings for workers at lower earnings levels. For example, benefits for someone who earned about 45 percent of the average wage and then retired at age 65 in 2010 replace about 55 percent of his or her prior earnings. But benefits for a person who always earned the maximum taxable amount—while higher in dollar terms—replace only 28 percent of his or her prior earnings.

In recent years, fewer employers have been offering defined-benefit pension plans, which guarantee a certain benefit level upon retirement, and more employers are offering defined-contribution plans, which pay a benefit based on a worker's contributions and the rate of return they earn. Thus, for most workers, Social Security will be their only source of guaranteed retirement income that is not subject to investment risk or financial market fluctuations.

Once someone starts receiving Social Security, his or her benefits are automatically increased each year to keep pace with inflation, helping to ensure that people do not fall into poverty as they age. In contrast, most private pensions and annuities are not adjusted for inflation, or are only partly adjusted.

Social Security provides a foundation of retirement protection for people at all earnings levels.

Fact #3: Social Security provides a foundation of retirement protection for nearly every American, and its benefits are not means-tested.

Almost all workers participate in Social Security by making payroll tax contributions, and almost all elderly people receive Social Security benefits. The near-universality of Social Security brings many important advantages.

Social Security provides a foundation of retirement protection for people at all earnings levels. It encourages private pensions and personal saving because it isn't means-tested—in other words, it doesn't reduce or deny benefits to people if their current income or assets exceed a certain level. Social Security provides a higher annual payout for a dollar contributed than private retirement annuities because the risk pool is not limited to those who expect to live a long time, no funds leak out in lump-sum payments or bequests, and its administrative costs are much lower. Indeed, universal participation and the absence of means-testing make Social Security very efficient to administer. Administrative costs amount to only 0.9 percent of annual benefits, far below the percentages for private retirement annuities. Proposals to means-test Social Security would undercut many of those important advantages.

Finally, the universal nature of Social Security assures its continued popular and political support. Large majorities of Americans say that they don't mind paying for Social Security because they value it for themselves, their families, and millions of others who rely on it.

Social Security is important for children and their families as well as for the elderly.

Fact #4: Social Security benefits are modest.

Social Security benefits are much more modest than many people realize. In June 2010, the average Social Security retirement benefit was $1,170 a month, or about $14,000 a year. (The average disabled worker and aged widow received slightly less.) When the program's full retirement age was 65, Social Security checks (after deducting the premium for Medicare's Supplementary Medical Insurance) replaced about 39 percent of an average worker's pre-retirement wages—significantly less than similar programs in most other Western countries. That figure will gradually fall to about 31 percent over the next two decades because of the projected rise in Medicare premiums (as health care costs continue to outpace general inflation) and the further increase in the full retirement age—which has already risen to 66—to 67 over the 2017–2022 period.

Fact #5: Children have an important stake in Social Security.

Social Security is important for children and their families as well as for the elderly. About 6 million children under age 18 (8 percent of all U.S. children) lived in families that received income from Social Security in 2008. That number included over 3 million children who received their own benefits as dependents of retired, disabled, or deceased workers, as well as others who lived with parents or relatives who received Social Security benefits. In all, Social Security lifted 1.1 million children out of poverty in 2008.

Fact #6: Almost half of the elderly would be poor without Social Security. Social Security lifts 13 million elderly Americans out of poverty.

Without Social Security benefits, almost half of Americans aged 65 and older would have incomes below the poverty line, all else being equal. With Social Security benefits, only one-tenth of the elderly do. The program lifts 13 million elderly Americans out of poverty.

Almost 90 percent of people aged 65 or older receive some of their family income from Social Security. Those not receiving Social Security mostly comprise recent immigrants, state and local government retirees (and federal retirees hired before 1984) who are covered by separate retirement systems, people under age 66 with significant earnings, and people who are so seriously disabled that they never worked and also have never married.

Fact #7: Most elderly beneficiaries rely on Social Security for the majority of their income.

For more than half (55 percent) of elderly beneficiaries, Social Security provides the majority of their cash income. For one-quarter (26 percent), it provides nearly all (more than 90 percent) of their income. For 15 percent of elderly beneficiaries, Social Security is the sole source of retirement income. Dependence on Social Security increases with age, as older people are less likely to work and more likely to have depleted their savings. Among those aged 80 or older, Social Security provides the majority of family income for 64 percent of beneficiaries and nearly all of the income for 33 percent of beneficiaries.

Fact #8: Social Security is particularly important for African Americans and Hispanics.

A person's race and ethnicity do not affect his or her Social Security eligibility or benefit levels. However, Social Security is a particularly important source of income for groups with low earnings and with less opportunity to save and earn pensions, including African Americans and Hispanics. Among beneficiaries aged 65 and older, Social Security represents 90 percent or more of income for 25 percent of whites, 34 percent of blacks, and 33 percent of Hispanics.

Blacks and Hispanics benefit substantially from Social Security because, on average, they have higher rates of disability and lower lifetime earnings than whites. Hispanics also have longer average life expectancies than whites, which means that they have more years to collect retirement benefits. Blacks are much more likely to benefit from survivors insurance. In 2007, African Americans made up 12 percent of the population, but 20 percent of children receiving Social Security survivor benefits were African American.

Fact #9: Social Security is especially beneficial for women.

Because women tend to earn less than men, take more time out of the paid workforce, live longer, accumulate less savings, and receive smaller pensions, Social Security is especially important for them. Women constitute 56 percent of Social Security beneficiaries aged 62 and older and 68 percent of beneficiaries aged 85 and older.

Alarmists who claim that Social Security won't be around when today's young workers retire either misunderstand or misrepresent the projections.

Women pay 40 percent of Social Security payroll taxes but receive 49 percent of Social Security benefits. This is because women benefit disproportionately from the program's inflation-protected benefits (because women tend to live longer), its progressive formula for computing benefits (because they tend to have lower earnings), and its benefits for non-working spouses and survivors.

Fact #10: Social Security can pay full benefits through 2037 without any changes, and relatively modest changes would place the program on a sound financial footing for 75 years and beyond.

Social Security's costs will grow in coming years as members of the large Baby Boom generation (those born between 1946 and 1964) move into their retirement years. Since the mid-1980s, however, Social Security has collected more in taxes and other income each year than it pays out in benefits and has amassed a trust fund of $2.6 trillion. The trust fund will enable Social Security to keep paying full benefits through 2037 without any changes in the program, according to Social Security's trustees, even though it starts paying out more in benefits than it receives in annual tax revenue before then.

After 2037 the trust fund will be exhausted if no changes are made. After that time, Social Security will be able [to] pay three-fourths of its scheduled benefits using its annual tax revenue. Alarmists who claim that Social Security won't be around when today's young workers retire either misunderstand or misrepresent the projections.

The long-term gap between Social Security's projected income and promised benefits is estimated at 0.7 percent of gross domestic product (GDP) [a measure of the nation's total economic output] over the next 75 years (and 1.4 percent of GDP in 2084). By coincidence, that roughly matches the revenue loss over the next 75 years from extending the Bush tax cuts for people making over $250,000. Members of Congress cannot simultaneously claim that the tax cuts for the richest 2 percent of Americans are affordable while the Social Security shortfall constitutes a dire fiscal threat.

A mix of tax increases and modest benefit reductions— carefully crafted to shield the neediest recipients and give ample notice to all participants—could put the program on a sound financial footing indefinitely. As Social Security marks its 75th birthday, policymakers have an opportunity to reassure future generations that they, too, can count on this successful program.

Social Security: A Target Without a Cause

David R. Francis

David R. Francis is a financial journalist whose "Economic Scene" column first appeared in The Christian Science Monitor *in 1964.*

Before President [Barack] Obama's State of the Union message Jan. 25 [2011], Social Security supporters were "really scared," as one Washington pundit put it. They worried that Mr. Obama would suggest cutting Social Security benefits as a way to trim the massive federal deficit. One liberal analyst, Robert Naiman, even called for citizens to occupy the offices and dog public events of members of Congress who refused to protect the program.

It turned out that Mr. Naiman's "jihad," as he called it, wasn't needed. The president's Social Security proposal is relatively mild and vague. He called for strengthening Social Security for future generations.

But Social Security remains a target of some conservative Republicans. Rep. Paul Ryan of Wisconsin, the new chairman of the House Budget Committee, states that Social Security is "going broke"; that it faces a $5.4 trillion deficit over the next 75 years, an amount equal to more than one-third of the annual size of the US economy. He maintains that if nothing is done, beneficiaries will face "a painful 22 percent across-the-board benefit cut" in 2037 when the Social Security trust fund is exhausted.

His message: Cut Social Security before cuts are forced on it. Partially privatize it, Mr. Ryan has further suggested. In other words, Social Security is a good place to cut even if it is not the cause of huge projected federal budget deficits.

Social Security remains the nation's most effective anti-poverty program.

Liberals offer a different view. Social Security benefits are modest, notes Kathy Ruffing, a policy analyst at the Center on Budget and Policy Priorities in Washington. Retired workers, disabled workers, and aged widows receive an average of only about $14,000 a year. More than 95 percent of recipients get less than $2,000 a month.

Moreover, most beneficiaries have little significant income from other sources. Corporate pensions have dwindled. Even with Social Security, median household income for all elderly beneficiaries is only about $20,000 a year. Further, Social Security benefits in the United States are low compared with government pensions of other advanced countries. If Social Security pensions in the US are compared with the government pensions provided by other relatively rich nations in the Organization for Economic Cooperation and Development on the basis of what proportion of preretirement earnings are replaced, the US ranks 26th out of 30. An average worker earning $43,000 in 2010 dollars will find that Social Security will replace only about 37 percent of his preretirement earnings on retirement at 65, calculates Ms. Ruffing. Raising the retirement age, as is often proposed to ease the program's coming deficit, means, in effect, an across-the-board cut in lifetime benefits.

Social Security remains the nation's most effective anti-poverty program. Without it, official poverty rates would rise from an already embarrassing 14.3 percent of Americans to about 23.7 percent, calculates the Economic Policy Institute. Social Security administrative costs are about a tenth that of private insurance companies.

So what's the answer for the program's way-in-the-future deficit?

The best remedy, economists agree, would be a thriving economy. It would boost payroll tax revenues automatically. If still needed, Social Security taxes could be hiked a bit.

But in 2037, benefits paid from payroll tax revenues alone will still be higher in real purchasing power than benefits today.

Social Security Is One of the Best Tools for Fighting Poverty Around the World

Claire Provost

Claire Provost works on The Guardian's *global development website, with special interests in open data, political economy, and participatory politics. The Guardian is a British national daily newspaper.*

With public spending on the chopping block around the world, a new UN [United Nations] report argues that social security is not only one of the most effective tools to reduce poverty and tackle inequality, but that it is also globally affordable.

Social Insecurity and the Need for Government Aid

Some 80% of the world's population lives in "social insecurity, unable to enjoy a set of social guarantees that enable them to deal with life's risks", according to the report. For Michael Cichon, the director of the International Labour Organisation's social security programme, the "scandal" is that only 2% of global gross domestic product (GDP) [a measure of a country's total economic output] would be needed to provide basic social security to all of the world's poor.

Launched in New York last week [February 14, 2011], in advance of the World Day of Social Justice, on Sunday, the report says that effective social security can help countries "grow with equity" from the earliest stages of their economic development, and that the "we can't afford it" argument simply falls flat. "All we need in developing country context is 4% GDP to reduce the poverty rate in a country by about 14 per cent," says Cichon.

The report, which is a joint effort by the United Nations Development Programme and the ILO [International Labour Organisation], surveys successful social protection programmes from developing countries—most of them from South America—seeking to enhance the multi-agency UN effort to promote a global "social protection floor".

While many of the traditional donor countries are rolling back on social expenditures, to cut deficits and finance fiscal stimulus packages, the report finds that developing countries are establishing innovative ways to provide social security. "The real innovation these days comes from the global South," says Cichon.

Among the findings:

- Argentina's universal child allowance programme, Asignación Universal por Hijo, covers 85% of Argentine children and is credited with reducing poverty by 22% and extreme poverty by 42%;

- Brazil's Bolsa Familia conditional cash transfer scheme covers 26% of the population, 50 million people, and has contributed one third to the decline in income inequality over the past decade. It is the biggest social transfer scheme in the world;

- Mexico's Oportunidades conditional cash-transfer programme reaches 25% of the population; it has helped to increase medical check-ups, contributing to an 11% reduction in maternal mortality and a 2% reduction in infant mortality, including other gains in education and nutrition;

- South Africa's Child Support Grants reach 10 million children and reduce the poverty gap by 28.3%;

- Thailand's universal health care scheme reaches 80% of the population and, by 2008, it had prevented 88,000 households from falling below the poverty line.

Other cases include: universal pension schemes in Bolivia, Equador and Thailand, basic health care programmes in China and Colombia, rural social insurance and employment programmes in Brazil and India, and early experiences in developing social protection schemes in Burkina Faso, Cambodia, Mozambique and Rwanda.

The Debate on Best Practices

Innovative forms of social protection, especially the increasingly popular conditional, cash-transfer schemes, are being promoted as low-cost ways to reach the poor and achieve "growth with equity". Chile's Solidario programme, for example, runs at a cost of about 0.1% of the country's GDP. Similarly large-scale, national programmes such as Mexico's Oportunidades and Brazil's Bolsa Familia come with price-tags of 0.4% of GDP.

Debates, however, do continue about the structure of these schemes. Should cash transfers, for example, be given universally or should they be targeted to certain sectors of the population? Should they be given out with no special demands attached, or should they be tied to certain conditions, such as bringing your child to school?

While it might make sense to give out larger grants to a smaller number of people, rather than smaller grants to a larger number, there is little evidence that conditions have any actual impact.

This was the controversial thesis of *Just Give Money to the Poor: The Development Revolution from the Global South*, a book published last year [2010] in which Joseph Hanlon, Armando Barrientos, and David Hulme argue that poorer people use money wisely when given it directly, sending their children to schools, starting businesses, and feeding their families. Pegged as a direct challenge to an ever-complex and bureaucratic aid industry, the authors say that letting the poor decide themselves how to use their money, bypassing governments and NGOs [nongovernmental organizations], is the hidden development revolution already under way.

The multi-agency UN effort to revive debate on best practices in social protection comes in advance of an ILO meeting in June this year, where member states will gather alongside workers' and employers' associations to draw up a long-term social protection strategy. Set to establish a "social protection floor", the strategy will address basic income security for children, social assistance for the unemployed, pensions and universal healthcare.

Social Security Is Not a Ponzi Scheme

Los Angeles Times

The Los Angeles Times *is a daily newspaper published in Los Angeles, California.*

The conventional wisdom has long held that Social Security is the "third rail" of politics, so popular that criticizing it amounts to committing political suicide. Evidently no one bothered to warn Texas Gov. Rick Perry, who repeated his critique that Social Security is a "Ponzi scheme" shortly after entering the race for the Republican presidential nomination. His hyperbolic denunciation, which has resonated with segments of the GOP [the Republican Party] and the "tea party" movement, reflects some of the real problems in the 76-year-old program. But it misconstrues what those problems are and how they can be fixed.

A Misunderstanding of Social Security

Perry contends that it's a "monstrous lie" to tell young workers that Social Security is still going to be around when they retire. Never mind that Congress has periodically raised the payroll tax and adjusted the benefit formula to put the program back on solid ground. The fact that actuaries identify new threats to its long-term health seemingly every decade feeds the suspicion that there's something fundamentally wrong.

The suspicion stems in part from a misunderstanding about what Social Security is. It's not a retirement savings program; it's an insurance plan designed to help the elderly, the disabled and their families stay out of poverty. And unlike a savings program's returns, there isn't a direct relationship between what workers pay into Social Security and what they get out of it. Instead, those who had high salaries receive a smaller percentage of their average wages than those who worked in low-paying jobs.

The [1983 payroll tax] increases were supposed to prepare for the retirement of the baby boom generation—an unusually large group whose numbers threatened to overwhelm the program.

As with many insurance plans, Social Security is set up primarily as a pay-as-you-go system. Current workers' contributions are mainly used to fund current retirees' benefits. Here's the problem. The program was created in an era with high birthrates and a steady influx of new workers. As a result, there were far more workers contributing to the system than there were receiving benefits. That ratio of workers to retirees has declined over the years, increasing the cost pressure on younger workers. But other factors—such as shifting workforce patterns, wage growth and immigration—have reduced that pressure.

Congress responded to the demographic changes by increasing Social Security tax rates 20 times and the maximum amount of wages subject to the tax 43 times between 1937 and 2009, as well as gradually raising the age at which recipients could start collecting full retirement benefits. Benefits increased too, but there was no escaping the fact that later generations had to pay more for their Social Security benefits than their predecessors had.

A Need to Adjust Social Security Again

The last major set of changes in the payroll tax, which were enacted in 1983, were designed to kill two birds with one stone. In addition to fixing a short-term shortfall, the increases were supposed to prepare for the retirement of the baby boom generation—an unusually large group whose numbers threatened to overwhelm the program. For about 20 years, the system would build up trillions of dollars in reserves by collecting more from workers than the program paid out in benefits. The reserves would then help pay for the boomers' benefits.

Those changes were supposed to put the program on a sound financial footing for 75 years. By the mid-1990s, however, it became clear that Congress hadn't gone far enough. The latest projection is that the program will fall $6.5 trillion short over the coming 75 years. That's not because of the dwindling ratio of workers to retirees, however. An advisory panel reported in 1997 that lawmakers had correctly factored in that change. Instead, the main problems have been slower wage growth and larger disability benefit costs than anticipated, as well as the limitations of trying to measure a host of variables 75 years into the future.

In other words, Social Security isn't built on a faulty foundation. It does, however, need regular adjustments to keep the tax and benefit formulas in line. As the advisory panel noted in 1997, Congress needs to adjust it again—by broadening its tax base, increasing payroll taxes, raising the retirement age, reducing the annual increases in benefits or some combination thereof. The longer it waits to do so, the larger the adjustments will have to be.

Even if lawmakers do nothing, the Social Security program would soldier on indefinitely, albeit at a reduced level. The Social Security Trust Fund (currently valued at more than $2.6 trillion) would keep growing for about a decade, largely thanks to the interest it accumulates. Then it would help maintain the current rate of benefit growth until about 2036. Once the trust fund was exhausted, the benefits for retirees would fall sharply; payroll taxes would generate only enough money to pay 77% of the benefits owed under the current formula.

Even at that level, benefits should be at least as large for most retirees as the ones paid to retirees today. But such a sharp reduction would be unconscionable, considering how many Americans rely on Social Security just to get by. The program's monthly checks account for at least 90% of the income received by more than a third of today's 54 million beneficiaries.

The Social Security Trust Fund

Perry contends that the day of reckoning for Social Security is coming far sooner than 2036. In his view, the trust fund is filled with worthless IOUs because Congress borrowed the money to cover part of the cost of operating the government. Those IOUs take the form of special Treasury securities that can't be sold to the public; instead, the Treasury Department has to buy them back. That means the federal government will have to borrow the money needed to redeem the trust fund's holdings unless it cuts spending or raises taxes enough to create a budget surplus. That borrowing won't require an increase in the debt limit, though—the "intragovernmental debt" owed to the trust fund is already included in the amount subject to the limit.

So no, the Social Security Trust Fund isn't stuffed with cash. But the securities in the trust fund are backed by the full faith and credit of the United States, just like T-bills or any other federal bond. Defaulting on them would cause an order-of-magnitude more damage to the U.S. credit rating, and in turn its economy, than Washington's recent brinkmanship over raising the debt ceiling. Such a step would be unthinkable, but then, so was a major presidential candidate calling Social Security a Ponzi scheme.

Social Security Is Similar to a Ponzi Scheme

Michael Tanner

Michael Tanner is a senior fellow at the Cato Institute, a libertarian think tank. Tanner conducts research on domestic policies such as health care, social welfare, and Social Security.

Recently there has been much debate over whether Social Security is or is not a Ponzi scheme. . . .

The operator of the Ponzi scheme recruits "investors," promising high returns on their investment or contribution. But the operator does not actually invest the money, and instead pockets it for himself. Because no investments are made, the scheme's operator can only pay returns in one of two ways: 1) return a portion of the investment as "interest" or "profit," while convincing the investor to keep his principle invested; and 2) recruiting new investors and using their money to pay the earlier ones. However, these new investors will now have to be paid, requiring the operator to recruit a third round of investors large enough to pay for both the initial and secondary investors. This continues until the operator is no longer able to recruit sufficient new investors and the system ultimately collapses. . . .

Social Security as a Ponzi Scheme

Some defenders of the current system insist that Social Security cannot be a Ponzi scheme because, as *USA Today* editorialized, "Ponzi schemes are a criminal enterprise; Social Security is not." But this is simply a tautology that says nothing about the program's structure.

Michael Tanner, "Social Security, Ponzi Schemes, and the Need for Reform," *Policy Analysis*, vol. 689, November 17, 2011, pp. 1–10, 14. Copyright © 2011 by The Cato Institute. All rights reserved. Reproduced by permission.

Other defenders point out that Ponzi schemes are, by their very nature, fraudulent, making promises that the scheme's operator has no intention of keeping. Moreover, the operators lie about whether or not they are investing the participant's money. Social Security, on the other hand, they say, is transparent, honest about its structure, and honest about the benefits it will deliver. In one widely cited column, political blogger Jonathan Bernstein put it this way: "[S]aying that Social Security is a Ponzi scheme or is like a Ponzi scheme is basically a false accusation of fraud against the U.S. government and the politicians who have supported Social Security over the years."

In keeping with the earlier definition of a Ponzi scheme, Social Security does *promise benefits that the government knows it cannot deliver.*

Here, the program's defenders are on even shakier ground. While the Social Security Administration's website and official publications are indeed straightforward about how the program operates, many Americans still mistakenly believe that their Social Security taxes are somehow saved for their retirement. One only has to listen to any Social Security debate where seniors assert that they are "getting back what they paid into the system" to realize that many recipients are not clear on the program's financing. Social Security's use of terminology, such as "Trust Fund," has perpetuated much of this misunderstanding. Again, witness how many Americans believe that Social Security is in trouble because the government has spent, borrowed, or "looted" the money that should be in the Trust Fund. According to a recent Rasmussen poll, just 10 percent of voters know that Social Security taxes are not reserved for Social Security payments.

More significantly, in keeping with the earlier definition of a Ponzi scheme, Social Security *does* promise benefits that the government knows it cannot deliver. For example, if a worker uses the Social Security Administration's "Benefit Calculator," he or she will receive an estimate of his or her Social Security benefits under current law. However, given current levels of financing, the Social Security system cannot pay those benefits in full after 2037. In fact, by law, benefits would have to be reduced by 24 percent after that date.

Some defenders of Social Security suggest that the program shouldn't be compared to a Ponzi scheme because, unlike a Ponzi scheme, Social Security's purposes are beneficent.

From 1999 until March of 2011, this benefit estimate was mailed to workers annually. During the [George W.] Bush administration, the Personal Benefits Statement (PEBS) contained a disclaimer that:

> Your estimated benefits are based on current law. Congress has made changes to the law in the past and can do so at any time. The law governing benefit amounts may change because, by 2037, the payroll taxes collected will be enough to pay only about 76 percent of scheduled benefits.

This warning was discontinued when the Social Security Administration stopped mailing paper copies of the benefit statement, and it is not included in the online calculator. While the Social Security Administration website includes discussions of the program's financial problems elsewhere on the site, someone looking for what his or her benefits will be would not be told that Social Security cannot pay the listed benefit. And even during the Bush administration, the disclaimer was on a separate page of the PEBS from the listed benefit level, and buried within a lengthy text. Small print aside, the Social Security Administration is providing a misleading promise of benefits.

An Insurance Plan?

Defenders of Social Security also suggest that the investment structure of the program is irrelevant because Social Security resembles an "insurance" program more than it resembles an investment plan. As the *Los Angeles Times* puts it, "It's not a retirement savings program; it's an insurance plan designed to help the elderly, the disabled, and their families stay out of poverty." But even if one accepts the definition of Social Security as insurance, that is a description of benefits and how they are determined, not of financing.

Indeed, insurance companies "are required to maintain reserves and capital and surplus at all times and in such forms so as to provide an adequate margin of safety." All 50 states impose capital reserve requirements on insurers, guaranteeing their ability to pay claims. Typical is New York, which mandates, "Every insurer shall . . . maintain reserves in an amount estimated in the aggregate to provide for the payment of all losses or claims incurred." No insurance company could legally plan to fund future claims out of future premiums. An insurance company that did so would resemble a Ponzi scheme. Yet, that is very close to how Social Security promises to pay future claims to its benefits.

Beneficent Purposes?

Finally, some defenders of Social Security suggest that the program shouldn't be compared to a Ponzi scheme because, unlike a Ponzi scheme, Social Security's purposes are beneficent. As Perry's [Texas governor Rick Perry, who claimed Social Security is set up like an illegal Ponzi scheme] rival, former Massachusetts's governor Mitt Romney, says, the program is "a recognition that we want to care for those in need, and our seniors have the need of Social Security." But the implication of this argument is that, if Charles Ponzi had given his proceeds to charity, or if he had really believed that he could pay profits to his investors, there would have been no problem with his scheme. Clearly, intent and outcome are two different things.

None of these arguments deal with the underlying question of Social Security's financial structure. Even if one concedes that Social Security is a legal, transparent, and beneficent insurance scheme, if it is set up structurally as a Ponzi scheme it will ultimately fail. And it is in this structure that, with one important distinction, Social Security does indeed resemble a Ponzi scheme.

A Classic Ponzi Scheme

Social Security is a *pay-as-you-go* (PAYGO) program, in which Social Security taxes are used to immediately pay benefits for current retirees. It is not a *funded* plan, where contributions are accumulated and invested in financial assets and liquidated and converted into a pension at retirement. Rather, it is a simple wealth transfer from current workers to current retirees. . . .

The PAYGO program provides initial retirees a windfall because they never paid taxes into the system. Subsequent generations both pay taxes and receive benefits. There is no direct relationship between taxes paid and benefits received. As a result of this structure, Social Security resembles a classic Ponzi scheme in many aspects.

When Social Security was running a surplus, the excess revenues were used to purchase special-issue treasury bonds.

There is no investment. Like a Ponzi scheme, Social Security does not actually save or invest any of a participant's payments. When a worker pays taxes into the system, that money is used to pay current beneficiaries. Since Social Security began running a cash-flow deficit this year [2011], paying out more in benefits than it takes in through taxes, every dollar collected in Social Security taxes (and more) is used to pay benefits. There is no money left over to invest. And since Social Security is currently projected to never return to surplus, there will be no future investments.

However, what about the surplus Social Security taxes that accumulated in the Social Security Trust Fund from 1984 to 2010, a period when Social Security did collect slightly more in taxes than it paid in benefits? Could that have been considered as invested?

When Social Security was running a surplus, the excess revenues were used to purchase special-issue treasury bonds. When the bonds were purchased, the Social Security surplus became general revenue and was spent on the government's annual general operating expenses. What remained behind in the Trust Fund were the bonds, plus an interest payment attributed to the bonds. Currently the Trust Fund holds roughly $2.9 trillion in such bonds. Those bonds are, in essence, a form of IOU, a promise against future taxes. When the bonds become due, the government will have to repay them out of general revenue.

Since Trust Fund accumulations are spent like any other government revenue, the Social Security Trust Fund could be considered an investment to the degree that general government spending could be considered investment. But relatively little federal spending meets that definition, including infrastructure and some education spending. Most government spending is simply transfer payments or other forms of consumption. In fact, by the government's own estimates, only 15.7 percent of federal spending can be considered investments. Since the maximum Social Security surplus represented just 15 percent of Social Security taxes, an investment rate of less than 16 percent of federal spending means that less than 2.5 percent of Social Security taxes were ever invested in anything.

Taking a slightly different tack, others, such as Center for American Progress blogger Matthew Yglesias, argue that all Social Security taxes should be considered to have been invested in the U.S. economy as a whole, since recipients are ultimately relying on the fruits of that economy to pay their benefits. He claims that Social Security is similar to private pensions or even 401(k) plans in this sense. With stocks or other private investments, he writes:

> Your expectation is that at a future date . . . you'll be able to exchange those shares for money. More money than you paid for them in the first place. Why would that work? Well, it could work because you were just stupendously lucky. But the reason we anticipate that it will work *systematically* is that we anticipate that there will be economic growth. In the future, people will in general have more money, so assets will be more valuable.

Yglesias goes on to argue that the same can be said of Social Security:

> Its actuarial situation is just the same as a stock market investment in this regard. If future economic growth is lower than anticipated, it will be impossible to pay the anticipated level of benefits. On the other hand, if future economic growth is faster than anticipated, it would be possible to pay even more benefits than had been promised.

It is true that, whether you are talking stocks or Social Security, returns are ultimately a claim on the wealth produced by future generations. The future value of stocks, bonds, property, and other investments is ultimately dependent on future cash flows such as dividends, interest, and rents. They are, in turn, dependent on economic growth. If economic growth in the future is poor, the taxes available to pay Social Security will not be available, but asset values will likely also decline.

However, this analysis ignores the fact that in a dynamically efficient economy the rate of return on labor, the basis for the payroll taxes that will be used to pay future benefits, is lower than the rate of return on capital, the basis for investment returns. . . . In the United States the return on capital has generally run about 2.5 percentage points higher than the return on labor.

Yglesias's analysis also ignores the impact that private investment has on economic growth. Whereas, as shown above, Social Security is simply a transfer program, feeding consumption rather than investment, private pension programs *do* invest their contributions, thereby boosting economic growth. In fact, [economist] Martin Feldstein and others have suggested that Social Security's impact may actually be worse than no investment. Because individuals substitute Social Security for private savings, the program actually displaces savings and investment that would otherwise occur. Feldstein, for example, suggests that if the amount currently paid in Social Security taxes were instead invested privately, it would "increase the economic well-being of future generations by an amount equal to 5 percent of GDP [gross domestic product, a measure of total economic output] each year."

Early Participants Get a Windfall

Earlier investors win big. Like a Ponzi scheme, Social Security paid early participants a windfall return on their money. There are two reasons for this.

First, because individual Social Security taxes are not saved or invested for that individual's retirement, the Social Security benefits that the individual receives are not directly linked to the taxes paid. As the Supreme Court ruled in *Flemming v. Nestor* (1960), this means that people have no legal, contractual, or property right to benefits. Congress can change, reduce, or take away those benefits at any time. However, it also means that Congress can set a minimum benefit level that is also unrelated to contributions.

That is what Congress did in the case of Social Security's earliest recipients. As Edward Witte, executive director of Franklin Roosevelt's Committee on Economic Security, told the House Ways and Means Committee in 1935, if benefits were proportional to contributions:

> The man at $40 [in wages per month] will get a pension of around 20 cents a month after 5 years of contributions, which is such a small amount that it would not be considered satisfactory. . . . Although the actuaries may compute that his contributions would buy a monthly annuity of only 20 cents, he is apt to think that he has earned a pension of $10 or $15 at least. It is that psychological factor that you have to take into account. A pension of such a small amount as people who are in the system only a short time can buy, will never be satisfactory to them. It will seem to them that they are being cheated.

Congress therefore set an initial minimum monthly benefit of $10 for anyone who had paid into the system for at least five years. This meant that early beneficiaries received payments far in excess of any contributions. For example, the very first Social Security recipient, Ida Mae Fuller of Vermont, paid just $22.54 in Social Security taxes, but the long-lived Mrs. Fuller collected $22,888.92 in benefits.

Second, because the early stages of a PAYGO Social Security system, like the early stages of a Ponzi scheme, are characterized by a high ratio of contributors to beneficiaries, taxes can initially be set at artificially low rates.

Current Workers Expect a Poorer Rate of Return

Current recipients depend on recruiting subsequent recipients who receive lower returns. Like a Ponzi scheme, Social Security participants receive payments, not from returns on their own investments, but directly from inflows from subsequent participants. That means that, as in a Ponzi scheme, the system can only continue to provide benefits as long as it is able to recruit additional people to pay into it.

Social Security is squarely based on what has been called the eighth wonder of the world—compound interest.

Yet, the demographic changes described above mean that Social Security has not been able to maintain a sufficient number of taxpayers/contributors. Fewer contributors per beneficiary means that the initially low tax rates must rise faster than benefits, resulting in lower rates of return for subsequent participants who must pay more in taxes per dollar in benefits than earlier participants. As a result, the overall internal rates of return have declined steadily.

In theory, each generation's rate of return should be equal to the rate of growth in the wage base covered by the system. The growth of the wage base, in turn, is based on the growth in the labor force plus the growth in real wages. As long as the wage base continues to grow, Social Security can continue to yield a positive rate of return.

Calling Social Security "a Ponzi Scheme that works," [economist] Paul Samuelson summed up this point:

> The beauty of social insurance is that it is actuarially unsound. Everyone who reaches retirement age is given benefit privileges that far exceed anything he has paid in—exceed his payments by more than ten times (or five times counting employer payments)! How is it possible? It stems from the fact that the national product is growing at a compound interest rate and can be expected to do so for as far ahead as the eye cannot see. Always there are more youths than old folks in a growing population. More important, with real income going up at 3 percent per year, the taxable base on

which benefits rest is always much greater than the taxes paid historically by the generation now retired. Social Security is squarely based on what has been called the eighth wonder of the world—compound interest. A growing nation is the greatest Ponzi game ever contrived.

Samuelson would be correct if there were no demographic factors to consider. As long as the wage base supporting Social Security grows faster than the number of recipients, the program can continue to pay higher benefits to those recipients. But the growth in the labor force has slowed dramatically. In 1950, for example, there were 16 workers paying taxes into the system for every retiree receiving benefits from the program. However, Americans have been living longer and having fewer babies. As a result, there are now just 2.9 workers per beneficiary, and by 2020 there will be only two. And real wage growth . . . has not been nearly fast enough to offset this demographic shift.

Thus, as Michael Boskin of Stanford University explained, "While the percentage of transfers in benefits is largest for the first cohort of retirees (who receive virtually a complete windfall), the positive intergenerational transfers received by retirees . . . [eventually turns] negative for subsequent retirees." A worker earning the median wage who retired in 1984 earned an approximate internal return of 4 percent on his or her taxes. In contrast, a similar worker retiring this year can expect a return of 2.2 percent. If that worker were age 30 this year and planning to retire in 2037, he or she would hope to earn a return of just 1.5 percent.

Thus, not only can current workers expect a far poorer rate of return than that experienced by earlier participants, but the return they receive is far lower than the return to private capital investment.

In all these aspects, therefore, Social Security clearly resembles a Ponzi scheme. . . .

Reform Is Needed

However, unlike Charles Ponzi's scheme, Social Security will never go broke as long as the government can force people to pay more taxes and accept fewer benefits. In the end, that is the crucial difference. Social Security is not a Ponzi scheme because Charles Ponzi didn't have a gun.

Yet, Congress's ability to preserve Social Security through higher taxes and lower benefits should not distract from the more fundamental problem that the program's Ponzi-like structure makes it unable to pay currently promised levels of benefits with current levels of taxation. In short, the program is facing insolvency without fundamental reform. That reform should not just make young workers pay more and receive less. Rather, it should remove the Ponzi-like aspects of the program by allowing younger workers to save a portion of their payroll taxes through privately invested personal accounts.

A system of personal retirement accounts would be one that clearly is not a Ponzi scheme.

The Outcome for Social Security Is the Same as a Ponzi Scheme— Lower Future Benefits

Chuck Saletta

Chuck Saletta is a conservative columnist and political commentator and a frequent contributor to Motley Fool, a multimedia financial-services company and website.

Social Security's trust fund is in the process of collapsing because it will have insufficient funds available to pay promised benefits. Sound like a Ponzi scheme? That's what many prominent political and investing figures have called it.

Whether the system meets a broad definition of Ponzi scheme, at least this "scheme" is one in which you *can* come out ahead.

You've got a few things going for you:

- Charles Ponzi's original setup had a frightfully speedy collapse that occurred after around 200 days. Social Security currently estimates its trust fund won't run dry until around 2036.

- When Social Security's trust fund does empty, recipients will still get about three-quarters of their expected benefits. For contrast, just ask the victims of Bernie Madoff's Ponzi scheme how tough it is to get money out of a real Ponzi scheme after it collapses. [Madoff's multi-billion-dollar investment scam, the largest in US history, collapsed in December 2008.]

Chuck Saletta, "Ponzi Scheme or Not, Social Security Can't Keep Up the Pace," *Daily Finance*, January 13, 2012. Copyright © 2012 by AOL, Inc. All rights reserved. Reproduced by permission.

The Good News? You've Been Warned

You have time until Social Security's trust fund vanishes—meaning you can still prepare for that event. Even better, the best way to prepare is to essentially do what you should have been doing anyway: Invest for your retirement.

To prepare for Social Security's diminished capacity, you must ask yourself how much . . . you'll need to support your lifestyle in retirement.

Even if Social Security's trust fund weren't in trouble, the program generally replaces only about 40% of a person's average lifetime income, indexed for inflation. When Social Security's trust fund is gone and the program pays out reduced benefits, the typical recipient will get closer to 30% of average earnings.

Unless you're preparing to live on what amounts to a minimum wage salary you should already be investing heavily for your retirement.

Retire Comfortably Anyway

To prepare for Social Security's diminished capacity, you must ask yourself how much of your average earnings you'll need to support your lifestyle in retirement.

The general rule of thumb is somewhere in the 70% to 80% range, but circumstances vary from person to person. If you're figuring on 75%—the midpoint of that range—then what Social Security's troubles really mean is that you'll need to replace 45% of your salary from other sources. That's up from the 35% you'd have to cover with a healthy Social Security.

Viewed in that light, planning for the collapse of Social Security's trust fund becomes a fairly straightforward numbers game.

How to Make Up for Social Security's Coming Shortfall

Increasing the amount of income that needs to be replaced by your portfolio from 35% of salary to 45% requires just under 30% more money, all else being equal. That's not an insurmountable hurdle to clear, and it helps clarify the four levers you'll be working with to cover that gap. Those levers are:

1. *Save more*: If you can come up with a little bit more every paycheck to put toward your retirement, you can cover that gap. If money's a bit tight right now, you can choose to save part of your raises as soon as you get them. That way, you'll never miss the money you had never seen, while boosting your nest egg to cover your golden years.

2. *Work longer*: At around 8% returns, it'd take around three extra years of working to cover that gap, perhaps a bit less if you continue to sock away new contributions during that time. Of course, it could take you a bit longer or shorter, depending on both your investment choices and the market's mood. But if you have the option of staying on the job, it's a good way to make up for Social Security's shortfall.

3. *Seek higher returns*: If you invest a bit more aggressively, your portfolio may be able to grow a few percentage points faster. Those few points, compounded over several years, can add up to some serious coin—and enough to cover the gap. There are no guarantees in investing, however, and more aggressive investing does bring with it the potential for loss, as well as gain.

4. *Live with less*: Of course, if you do nothing differently in your retirement planning, you're currently scheduled to wind up with around a quarter less Social Security money once the trust fund is gone. If your general costs of living are low enough that you won't be materially affected by missing that money, then you can simply do without it.

Because there are still a couple of decades until the trust fund is gone, all four of those levers are at your disposal, as is the ability to use a combination of those levers to your advantage. The longer you wait to get started, though, the less valuable the investing-related levers will be. Wait long enough, and your choices will be limited to living with less or working longer before retiring.

Whether Social Security meets the technical definition of a Ponzi scheme, the net effect to you is the same. The trust fund is running out of money, and you need to plan for a retirement with a smaller Social Security check headed your way. Otherwise, 2036 will be here sooner than you think, and the decision will be made for you, instead of by you.

Social Security Is a Mandatory Ponzi Scheme That Is Bad for American Workers

Julie Borowski

Julie Borowski is a staff writer at FreedomWorks, an organization headquartered in Washington, DC, that promotes lower taxes, less government, and more freedom.

[T]exas governor] Rick Perry made headlines for calling Social Security a "Ponzi scheme" in last night's [September 5, 2011] presidential debate. [Former Massachusetts governor] Mitt Romney and statist media sources predictably attacked this position claiming that the insolvent program is A-Okay. To be fair, Rick Perry isn't the only Republican candidate with the courage to speak truth to fiction about Social Security. [Texas congressman] Ron Paul has likely been calling the entitlement program a Ponzi scheme long before I was even born. It's suddenly become popular to call Social Security out for what it really is, a compulsory Ponzi scheme.

Social Security is the definition of a Ponzi scheme with a few notable differences. Charles Ponzi started a money making scam that would later be known as a Ponzi scheme back in 1916. He persuaded people to allow him to invest their money but he never made one investment. He simply transferred money from his later investors to his earlier investors. The unsustainable system inevitably collapsed. Charles Ponzi was then convicted of fraud and spent years behind bars.

A Mandatory Ponzi Scheme

Social Security has many similarities to a Ponzi scheme but it's even worse. The main difference is that Ponzi schemes are voluntary and Social Security is mandatory. Everyone is forced to pay Social Security payroll taxes whether they want to be part of the system or not. Just like Charles Ponzi's fraudulent scheme, money from "later investors" or young workers is transferred to "earlier investors" or retirees.

Individuals should be free to opt-out of Social Security if they wish.

Ponzi schemes are always great for earlier investors but rip off those who invest later on. The number of retirees is growing far faster than the number of new workers. The ratio of workers to retirees has grown from 42 to 1 in 1940 to just 3.3 to 1 today. Social Security is facing more than $20 trillion in unfunded future liabilities. Young people actually believe that they have a better chance of seeing UFOs than a Social Security check made out to them when they retire.

Some people especially those on the left wrongly call us "cruel." But think about it: how cruel is it to force a young person who believes they will get nothing in return into a system? Why should young workers who are just starting out in their careers be forced to pay for the Social Security benefits of elderly millionaires and billionaires? Seniors are much wealthier than young people on average.

Individuals should be free to opt-out of Social Security if they wish. People could then stay in the insolvent Social Security system or invest on their own. If Social Security is so "great", why is it mandatory? Private sector retirement plans can provide safer plans with higher benefits than Social Security. Unlike Social Security, the assets in the private retirement plans can be rolled over to a surviving spouse or other family member. We need more retirement choices instead of being forced into a terribly mismanaged government monopoly. . . .

The Examiner's Tim Carney shows the difference between Ponzi schemes and Social Security. Bernie Madoff, who was responsible for the largest Ponzi scheme in history, was sentenced to 150 years in prison back in 2009. But the federal government's Social Security scheme is somehow mandatory. Politicians who criticize Social Security are indeed considered pariahs. *Think Progress* says that it is "nuts" to even compare Ponzi schemes and Social Security.

The Social Security scam disproportionately hurts the working class and African Americans. Tim Carney says that, "given that black men have a lower life expectancy, they get shortchanged on the benefits end." The life expectancy for an African American male is just 69.7 years—versus 75.5 years for white men. The Social Security retirement age is 65. This means that close to half of African American males will die before ever receiving a dime of Social Security benefits despite paying into the system all of their working life. How is *that* for cruel?

Social Security is a compulsory Ponzi scheme. As Cato Institute scholar Roger Pilon says, "a private company that ran such a scheme would be prosecuted in less than a New York minute." Social Security is a hopelessly bad deal for today's worker. Americans should be allowed to invest in their retirement as they see fit—not be forced into a mandatory Ponzi scheme against their will. We need more presidential candidates with the guts to propose allowing individuals to opt-out of Social Security.

CHAPTER 3

Would Private Retirement Accounts Be Better than the Current System?

Chapter Overview

Joe Messerli

Joe Messerli is the creator and author of almost all content on BalancedPolitics.org, a website designed to provide the public with a logical, balanced discussion on a number of important US political issues.

Due to the aging of the baby boom generation along with increased average life spans of American citizens, the current system of social security is headed for bankruptcy, meaning it will no longer generate the funds necessary to meet its obligations to retirees. Democrats and Republicans debate the actual timing of this insolvency, but no one disputes the fact that changes must be made eventually to keep the system going. Because the system is severely underfunded, one of two courses must be made at some point: 1) raise taxes to increase revenue generated, or 2) cut back on benefits paid out. Former President [George W.] Bush first popularized a new idea—private accounts.

Currently [May 2011], employees pay 6.2 percent in social security tax, which is matched by another 6.2 percent paid by the employer. Under several Republican plans (or rather their adaptation of an idea that's been used in Britain, Argentina, Australia, and Chile and proposed in the past by President [Bill] Clinton and Senate Minority leader Harry Reid), employees would be able to take a certain percent (e.g. 4 percent) and put it into a special private account they own, which the government can never touch (with the other 8.4 percent staying in the general trust fund). This private account could be invested in a number of mutual funds which could include stocks and bonds (in addition to no-risk investments such as treasury instruments). This private account would be transferable to next of kin upon death. Since investment in stocks and bonds are historically much higher than the return currently earned by the government system, advocates are convinced that the additional earnings of private investment will more than make up for the cutback in benefits.

Yes, Americans Should Be Able to Put Some of Their Social Security Contributions in Private Accounts

1. *It gives poor people a better chance to retire wealthy.* Americans living at the poverty level must usually spend every cent of their disposable income just to survive. Few in the lower-middle class have the funds available to put into a wealth-generating retirement account. Thus, they must rely on social security income to pay the bills when they reach retirement age. Unfortunately, the current social security payouts are at or below the poverty level. The money you earn in benefits based on what you pay in is less than what you'd earn in a passbook savings account. Talk to any person of wealth in this country. Do they have their money stuffed under a mattress? Is it in a taxable savings account earning 1 percent? Of course not. The majority of their money is going to be invested in stocks, bonds, real estate, and other wealth-building assets. The private accounts would provide a method of forced savings that would allow poorer people to participate in the advantages of stocks and bonds, allowing many to retire wealthy. For example, an individual or family that earns an average [annual income] of $30,000 during their working lifetime (age 18–65) will accumulate $213,743 in their private account based on a very conservative return of 5 percent. If they earn an average return of 10 percent

(which is close to the historical rate of return on the U.S. stock market), they will have accumulated $1,046,370 when they retire. That's right—a family making only $30,000 per year would retire as millionaires just based on the private accounts alone! Remember that the private account is only *part* of the benefits paid out by social security. The other 8.4 percent of taxes would go to the general trust fund which would be used to pay additional monthly benefits outside of the private account. In addition, Americans still have options outside of social security to invest for retirement—401(k)'s, IRA's [individual retirement accounts], pensions, and so on. Obviously there are no guarantees, but private accounts give every American a better opportunity to retire wealthy.

2. *It makes up for inevitable benefit cuts that must eventually be made to the system.* As many Americans are starting to become aware, the social security "trust fund" is not a diversified portfolio of assets waiting to be distributed to future retirees. It is a bucket of worthless government IOU's. Social security is based on a pay-as-you-go system. Social security taxes collected from current workers are used to pay benefits of current retirees. As the baby boom generation reaches retirement and life spans increase, the number of workers paying in will shrink while the number of retirees collecting benefits will increase. The system is currently not sustainable on its present course. This means taxes will have to rise or benefits will have to be cut. Tax increases are opposed by the Republican-controlled House since it could stifle a fragile economic recovery. Thus, benefits will have to be cut; i.e. the start age of benefits will have to be extended or the monthly check reduced. Private accounts would allow a larger accumulation of wealth

that will make up for the inevitable benefit cuts. In other words, new retirees can at least do as well as they currently are.

3. *The stock market should get an initial bump in value.* Over 60 percent of Americans currently own stock in some form, most notably in 401(k)'s, IRA's, and pension funds. The implementation of private accounts would mean more money would be injected into the stock market. Thus, by the laws of supply & demand, the market should go up in value.

4. *People are given a personal stake in the U.S. economy, providing extra incentive to help their companies and the nation as a whole to do well.* Many Americans feel disjointed from the success of their companies or the U.S. economy. In other words, if the stock market goes up or their company turns out record profits, they don't see an additional dime. They don't have a personal stake in the outcome. Thus, they are less likely to be motivated to do their best. After all, if they have no personal stake, it seems like they're just working to make rich people richer. The use of private retirement accounts would ensure that almost every American owned stock in some form. Thus, everyone would have a personal stake in the health of the U.S. economy. However small, this would lead to a greater motivation to give their best effort. More and more people would realize that the success of their company and the U.S. economy is good for everyone.

5. *Personal responsibility and ownership are injected into citizens' plans for retirement.* It is unfortunate that the revolution of government programs instituted by FDR [former president Franklin Delano Roosevelt] to help the less fortunate have led to a cradle-to-grave entitlement mentality. Too many Americans now believe that

the government owes them a living. They are less motivated to work and save because the government is always there to bail them out. The whole idea of former President Bush's "ownership society" was the philosophy that if people reap the rewards or suffer the consequences of their own actions, the maximum benefit for society is achieved. Think about it from the perspective of yourself only. If you didn't have social security (or other entitlement programs such as unemployment compensation), would you be more motivated to save and invest? Would you be more willing to work hard to ensure employment security and success? Would you be more willing to take a less-than-perfect job if you were laid off? Private accounts force people to take a good hard look at their retirement planning. In other words, it returns personal responsibility to a system that badly needs it. If you want to see the negative effects of an entitlement mentality, take a good look at the double-digit unemployment rates in social welfare-rich countries like France and Germany.

6. *Stocks & bonds are historically safe in long-term diversified portfolios (as evidence by their existence in every major government/union/corporate pension & retirement fund).* Any investment advisor will tell you that a diversified mix of stocks and bonds is very safe over the long term. Americans wouldn't have the option of withdrawing funds from their private social security accounts; thus, they'd be forced to invest long-term. In fact, almost every major government and union pension fund has a significant portion of its assets invested in stocks and bonds, which is the way its been done for almost a century. If stocks and bonds are so risky, why do almost all professional money managers continue to recommend them?

7. *Individuals who die early and don't recover all they paid in can pass on funds to their next of kin.* A person who earns an average of $40,000 during their working life (age 18–65) will pay a total of $233,120 in social security taxes after you add in the business share. If that money had been invested in conservative investments that earned 5 percent, you'd have $883,472 by the age of 65. At a 10 percent return, that person would accumulate $4,324,995 by age 65! How much does that person get if he dies before collecting his benefits? Zero. The money belongs to the government. He has no power to leave it to charity or put it in a trust fund for a grandchild's college. Under the private account plan, you would *own* the money in your private account. The government could never touch it, and you'd be allowed to dispose of it in your estate just like any other asset.

8. *Billions of dollars will be injected into corporate investment, leading to an economic stimulus.* Every economist will tell you that the key to growth is new investment. Economic growth leads to lower unemployment, lower inflation, and a greater standard of living for society as a whole. The implementation of private accounts would mean a significant amount of money would be invested into the private sector. And since money could be shifted around, the most efficient and successful companies would gain additional investment funds. One of the best "leading indicators" of a successful U.S. economic upturn or downturn is the U.S. stock market. Experts almost unanimously agree that the stock market would go up with the use of private social security accounts. One of the foremost economic experts in the world is . . . [former Federal Reserve] Chairman Alan Greenspan; he happens to support the idea of private accounts.

No, Americans Should Not Be Able to Put Some of Their Social Security Contributions in Private Accounts

1. *Poor portfolio management could leave some retirees severely short of funds.* Although stocks and bonds have historically done well over the long term, as any investment advisor will tell you, past success isn't a guarantee of future success. At the turn of the millennium the Nasdaq lost over 60 percent of its value as a result of the "tech bubble burst". The Dow index, which includes 30 of the most stable and well-known companies in the country, lost 30 percent of its value. Ironically, a mutual fund made up of stocks from either index would be considered a "well-diversified portfolio". Indeed, the funds of younger workers would most likely be put into smaller growth stocks that make up most of Nasdaq. Thus, imagine a scenario where you spent 30 years accumulating $200,000 in a private account; then, in one bad year, the value of the account dropped to $80,000. This is precisely what would have happened five years ago if private social security accounts had been in place. Hopefully, investment managers have learned from the tech market burst. However, do we want to be risking our retirement livelihood? Another terrorist attack could occur, sending the market into a tailspin. Someone at or near retirement age doesn't have a lot of options if his/her funds are suddenly lost. The subprime mortgage crisis in 2009 caused the same type of catastrophic drop in the entire stock market.

2. *Wide stock market price fluctuations could leave large groups of retirees in dire straits if their retirement occurs during a downturn.* Most stock market experts will point out that the long-term return on stocks has always been positive, despite temporary setbacks now and then. In

other words, the market may go up 150 percent one decade, then down 50 percent the next, then up 60 percent the next, then down 25 percent the next. Overall, the return may be positive, but what happens to the retirees that hit age 65 during one of the downturns? Hopefully they were wise enough to gradually put most of their money in safer investments, but there's no guarantee they did the right thing. Consequently, the unlucky retirees may be forced to live with a much smaller nest egg than they planned. The Nasdaq index lost over 60 percent of its value five years ago. It may take 10 or 20 years for it to return to its high value. Unfortunately, the trading technology of today (online transactions, program trading, up-to-the-second information dissemination, etc.) have made the market extremely volatile, which is the very definition of risk.

3. *There are several less complicated fixes to social security available.* The money, time, and bureaucratic complexity of private accounts aren't worth the effort and risk when there are much less complicated fixes available. Among these are the following: *1) Remove or raise the cap on taxes subject to social security tax* (which currently hovers around $90,000); the social security tax is currently the only tax on income that's regressive. In other words, once your income exceeds $90,000, the more money you make, the less you pay in tax as a percent of income. For example, someone who makes $50,000 pays $6200, or 12.4 percent (including the business share). Someone who makes $100,000 pays about $11,000, or 11 percent. Someone who makes $200,000 also pays about $11,000, or 5.5 percent. *2) Extend the age that benefits begin to be paid out.* When social security was first put in place, the average life span was about 67 years. Now, it's in the high 70s and continues to grow. For practical purposes, the age needs to be extended. *3)*

Use a hybrid of methods such as cutting benefits for upper income individuals, raising the amount of benefits subject to income tax, extending the cap on taxes subject to social security taxes, and so on. A bipartisan effort working with a set of economic experts should be able to craft some kind of effective, less risky plan.

4. *This isn't the best time to address the problem (i.e. there are far more urgent issues).* We have several decades to address the social security problem. In the middle of the War on Terror, with tension in Iraq, North Korea, Iran, Libya, Afghanistan, and Syria—in a time of trillion dollar deficits, this is not the best time to tackle the problem.

5. *Even more money will be taken out of an already underfunded system.* We all know that the social security system is severely underfunded; it's headed for bankruptcy sometime in the 2040s. Implementing private accounts will take 4 percent of the 12.4 percent taxes from every worker out of the trust fund. Thus, almost a 3rd of the revenue generated by social security taxes will be removed. Drastic benefit cuts or increased taxes will have to occur even sooner, which is a recipe for disaster.

6. *Current IRA's and 401k's offer essentially the same benefits as social security private accounts.* All of [the] financial benefits of private accounts—market investment, estate transferability, etc.—are already available in existing retirement investment vehicles. The main reason these options were set up in the first place was to supplement the social security system. Setting up private social security accounts will essentially provide a certain amount of redundancy, which isn't worth the cost and risk.

7. *The transition costs of setting up private accounts would be prohibitively high and severely add to an exploding*

deficit. As previously discussed, almost a 3rd of revenue generated from social security taxes would be removed immediately. In addition, the tax and bureaucratic headache of setting up such a system would be a nightmare. The transition costs of setting up private accounts could add over a trillion dollars to a deficit that is already at a $1.5 trillion-per-year level. This is way too much of a burden to leave future generations.

Personal Savings Accounts Would Provide Real Reform for Social Security

Dan Mitchell

Dan Mitchell is a senior fellow at the Cato Institute, a libertarian think tank, and an expert on fiscal policy issues.

There are two crises facing Social Security. First, the program has a gigantic unfunded liability, largely caused by demographics. Second, the program is a very bad deal for younger workers, making them pay record amounts of tax in exchange for comparatively meager benefits. . . . Personal accounts can solve both problems, and . . . nations as varied as Australia, Chile, Sweden, and Hong Kong have implemented this pro-growth reform.

Personal Accounts—The Right Approach

Social Security reform received a good bit of attention in the past two decades. President [Bill] Clinton openly flirted with the idea, and President [George W.] Bush explicitly endorsed the concept. But it has faded from the public square in recent years. But this may be about to change. Personal accounts are part of Congressman Paul Ryan's Roadmap proposal, and recent polls show continued strong support for letting younger workers shift some of their payroll taxes to individual accounts.

Equally important, the American people understand that Social Security's finances are unsustainable. They may not

Dan Mitchell, "The Case for Social Security Personal Accounts," *International Liberty*, January 10, 2011. Copyright © 2011 by Dan Mitchell. All rights reserved. Reproduced by permission.

know specific numbers, but they know politicians have created a house of cards, which is why jokes about the system are so easily understandable.

President [Barack] Obama thinks the answer is higher taxes, which is hardly a surprise. But making people pay more is hardly an attractive option, unless you're the type of person who thinks it's okay to give people a hamburger and charge them for a steak.

We're in a deep hole, but it will be easier to climb out if we implement real reform.

Other nations have figured out the right approach. Australia began to implement personal accounts back in the mid-1980s, and the results have been remarkable. The government's finances are stronger. National saving has increased. But most important, people now can look forward to a safer and more secure retirement. Another great example is Chile, which set up personal accounts in the early 1980s. . . . All told, about 30 nations around the world have set up some form of personal accounts. Even Sweden, which the left usually wants to mimic, has partially privatized its Social Security system.

Economic Benefits

It also should be noted that personal accounts would be good for growth and competitiveness. Reforming a tax-and-transfer entitlement scheme into a system of private savings will boost jobs by lowering the marginal tax rate on work. Personal accounts also will boost private savings. And Social Security reform will reduce the long-run burden of government spending, something that is desperately needed if we want to avoid the kind of fiscal crisis that is afflicting European welfare states such as Greece.

Last but not least, it is important to understand that personal retirement accounts are not a free lunch. Social Security is a pay-as-you-go system, so if we let younger workers shift their payroll taxes to individual accounts, that means the money won't be there to pay benefits to current retirees. Fulfilling the government's promise to those retirees, as well as to older workers who wouldn't have time to benefit from the new system, will require a lot of money over the next couple of decades, probably more than $5 trillion.

That's a shocking number, but it's important to remember that it would be even more expensive to bail out the current system. . . . We're in a deep hole, but it will be easier to climb out if we implement real reform.

Private Retirement Accounts Would Produce Much Higher Returns than Social Security

William G. Shipman and Peter Ferrara

William G. Shipman is cochairman of the Project on Social Security Choice, part of the Cato Institute, a conservative think tank that proposes public policies based on individual liberty, limited government, free markets, and peaceful international relations. Peter Ferrara is director of entitlement and budget policy at the Institute for Policy Innovation, another conservative think tank.

As Democrats and Republicans jockey to set Congress's agenda for after the [2010] midterm elections, President [Barack] Obama has already dismissed one reform that would improve Americans' financial standing: allowing workers to save and invest some of their Social Security taxes in personal accounts.

That's an "ill-conceived" proposal, Mr. Obama said in August, because it means "tying your benefits to the whims of Wall Street traders and the ups and downs of the stock market." The financial crisis, he said, should have put this idea to rest "once and for all."

A Safe and Lucrative Idea

Missing from the president's statements is any acknowledgment that, to date, all proposals to create personal accounts have provided workers with the option to invest for retirement or to stay with Social Security. Any worker could choose to reject the option. So, contrary to the president's assertion, creating personal accounts wouldn't suddenly empower those who "would gamble your Social Security on Wall Street."

> *By the time of their retirement in 2009, Joe and Mary would have accumulated account funds, after administrative costs, of $855,175.*

In addition, no proposal has required workers to invest personal account funds in Wall Street stocks, as opposed to other investments such as corporate or government bonds, bond mutual funds or indexes, or certificates of deposit.

Suppose a senior citizen—let's call him "Joe the Plumber"—who retired at the end of 2009, at age 66, had been able to set up a personal account when he entered the work force in 1965, at the age of 21. Suppose that, paying into his personal account what he and his employer would have paid into Social Security, Joe was foolish enough to invest his entire portfolio in the stock market for all 45 years of his working career. How would he have fared in the recent financial crisis?

While working, Joe had earned the average income for full-time male workers. His wife Mary, also age 66, had earned the average income for full-time female workers. They invested together in an indexed portfolio of 90% large-cap stocks and 10% small-cap stocks, which earned the returns reported each year since 1965.

By the time of their retirement in 2009, Joe and Mary would have accumulated account funds, after administrative costs, of $855,175. Indeed, they would have been millionaires a few years earlier, but the financial crisis lost them 37% in 2008. They were unfortunate to retire just one year after the worst 10-year stock market performance since 1926. Yet their account, having earned a 6.75% return annually from 1965 to 2009, would still pay them about 75% more than Social Security would have.

What's more, this model assumes that in retirement Joe and Mary switch to a lower-risk, conservative portfolio that averages a return of just 3%. Of course for young workers today, Social Security promises even lower returns of only 1.5% or less, given the actuarial value of all promised benefits. For many, the promised returns are zero or negative. And if Congress raises taxes or cuts benefits in order to close financial gaps—as everyone who rejects personal accounts effectively advocates—the eventual returns for young workers will be even lower.

It is a mathematical fact that the least expensive way to provide for an almost certain future liability is to save and invest in capital markets prior to the onset of the liability. That's why state and local pension funds, corporate pension plans, federal employee retirement plans and Chile's successful Social Security personal accounts (since copied by other countries) do so. It is sound practice.

And it's why Mr. Obama is wrong to assert that personal Social Security accounts are "ill-conceived," and why each of us should have the liberty to opt into one.

Personal Retirement Accounts Would Be No More Risky than Social Security

Michael Tanner

Michael Tanner is a senior fellow at the Cato Institute, a libertarian think tank. Tanner conducts research on domestic policies such as health care, social welfare, and Social Security.

Opponents of allowing younger workers to privately invest a portion or their Social Security taxes through personal accounts have long pointed to the supposed riskiness of private investment. The volatility of private capital markets over the past several years, and especially recent declines in the stock market, have seemed to bolster their argument. . . .

Given Social Security's ongoing financial problems and its inability to pay currently promised benefits, personal accounts remain an important and viable option for reforming the troubled system. It is important, therefore, to carefully examine market performance and compare that performance with Social Security benefits.

Social Security's Failing Finances

Although Social Security reform has largely been off the political radar since President George W. Bush's failed attempt to reform the system in 2004, the problems facing our national retirement system have not gone away. In fact, since the demise of the Bush proposal, Social Security's long-term unfunded liabilities have increased by nearly $6 trillion, to roughly $21 trillion. This year [2012], Social Security actually began running a cash-flow deficit, paying out more in benefits than it takes in through taxes.

Michael Tanner, "Still a Better Deal: Private Investment vs. Social Security," *Policy Analysis*, No. 692, February 13, 2012, pp. 2–7, 10. Copyright © 2012 by The Cato Institute. All rights reserved. Reproduced by permission.

In theory, of course, Social Security is supposed to continue paying benefits by drawing on the Social Security Trust Fund until 2036, after which the fund will be exhausted. At that point, *by law*, Social Security benefits will have to be cut by approximately 24 percent.

It would make sense . . . [to allow] younger workers the option of saving and privately investing . . . a portion of their Social Security taxes.

However, in reality, the Social Security Trust Fund is not an asset that can be used to pay benefits. Any Social Security surpluses accumulated to date have been spent, leaving a Trust Fund that consists only of government bonds that will eventually have to be repaid by taxpayers. . . .

On the other side of the ledger, restoring the program to solvency would require at least a 24 percent reduction in benefits. Suggested changes include further raising the retirement age, trimming cost-of-living adjustments, means-testing, or changing the wage-price indexing formula. Obviously, there are better and worse ways to make these changes. But any of those changes would ultimately mean that today's young workers would end up paying more, getting less, or both. Since Social Security's rate-of-return, just 2.2 percent for a middle-income earner retiring in 2012, is already far below the historic average for private capital markets, these changes would make Social Security an even worse deal for young workers. Since 1928, a period including the Great Depression, World War II, the stagflation of the 1970s, the bursting of the dot-com bubble, and the recent recession, the average annual real return on stocks in the U.S has been 6.09 percent.

It would make sense, therefore, to offset these changes by allowing younger workers the option of saving and privately investing at least a portion of their Social Security taxes. That would allow those workers to take advantage of the potentially higher returns available from capital investment. In a dynamically efficient economy, the return on capital will exceed the rate of return to labor, and therefore will be higher than the benefits that Social Security can afford to pay. In the United States, the return on capital has generally run about 2.5 percentage points higher than the return on labor.

On the other hand, capital markets are both risky and volatile. . . . Clearly, there has been a high degree of volatility, with the market making large swings down as well as up. However, despite those downturns, the S&P averaged an annual real return of 6.85 percent over the period.

At the same time, bonds were far less volatile, though there were still periods of negative returns. Over the past 40 years, government bonds averaged an average real annual return of 2.44 percent, while corporate bonds averaged 3.46 percent. An individual who combined the two would have seen an average annual real return of 2.93 percent.

Finally, it should be noted that bond and stock returns tend to move in opposition to each other. When stocks decline, bond returns tend to rise. This means that a mixed portfolio, combining investment in both stocks and bonds, can help mitigate risk.

Allowing younger workers to privately invest a portion of their Social Security taxes would expose them to a degree of risk. Effectively, they would be trading the political risk of an underfunded Social Security system for the market risk of private investment.

Opponents of personal accounts suggest that this market risk would inherently leave those workers worse off. But would it?

Private Investment vs. Social Security

In 2005, scholars at the Cato Institute [a conservative think tank] proposed a Social Security reform plan that would have phased out government-provided retirement benefits while allowing younger workers the option to privately invest half of their payroll taxes (6.2 percent of covered wages) through personal accounts. While the proposal would not have affected benefits for individuals 55 or older, and would have been gradually phased in on a voluntary basis for younger workers, eventually workers would have relied on the funds in their personal accounts for their entire retirement income.

Given the recent poor performance by private capital markets, what would have happened to workers who chose to invest privately rather than relying on Social Security? Since it is impossible to predict future investment returns, the best way to make this comparison is to look backward in time, assuming that the Cato plan had been in effect over the last 40 years.

For purposes of this experiment, let us posit three hypothetical individuals each of whom retired on November 7, 2011. One is a high-income worker whose last salary was equivalent to the 2011 Social Security salary cap of $106,800. The second is a middle-income worker whose final salary was equal to the median U.S. household income of $49,445. And, the last was a low-income worker who earned half the median income of $24,723.

Each of these workers was assumed to have begun working in 1968. In order to keep their wages consistent over time, their wages were backed down from current levels each year by the rate of average U.S. wage growth. Thus, when the high-income worker began work, he earned $11,662; the middle-income worker earned made $6,300; and the low-income worker earned $3,100.

Each worker was assumed to have taken advantage of the personal account option under the Cato proposal, and contributed half of the Social Security payroll tax each year to their private account, with the remainder of the payroll tax continuing into Social Security to help finance the transition, as well as to pay for survivors and disability benefits.

Investments were assumed to have been made on December 31 of each year, except for the final payment which was made on November 7, 2011. This lump-sum investment does somewhat oversimplify the model, since in reality the worker would be investing on each pay period, or roughly every two weeks. However, the tiny changes in returns over two-week periods would not significantly change the outcome.

Within the personal account, we assumed three possible investment portfolios. A high-risk/high-return portfolio consisting of 100 percent stocks; a medium-risk/medium-return portfolio of 50 percent stocks and 50 percent bonds, and a low-risk/low-return portfolio consisting entirely of bonds. Stock investments were assumed to be in an index reflecting returns to the S&P 500.

The worker [who set up private investment accounts] would always be better off than if he or she had received Social Security's rate of return.

For the bond fund, the investment package was comprised of 50 percent. U.S. Treasury bonds and 50 percent Moody's AAA corporate bonds. For the government bond component, the worker would invest in 10-year bonds annually, so there would be different cohorts of 10-year Treasury bonds maturing in successive years. This system of rolling annual contributions and the returns of maturing bonds into new 10-year bonds would continue until the last decade before retirement. Since, in order for the potential retirees to have all of their savings available upon retirement, they cannot invest in bonds that will mature after they retire, it was assumed that they invested in bonds with steadily decreasing years to maturity, telescoping from 10-year bonds down to 7-, 5-, and 3-year bonds.

From 2009 onward, it was assumed that new contributions to personal accounts simply remained in cash, since the yields on a one-year government bond are less than 1 percent, and the volatility of the stock market would argue against putting investing in stocks so close to retirement.

Administrative costs were assumed to equal 25 basis points, which was assessed each year on December 31. This is consistent with estimates made by the Social Security Administration's actuaries in scoring private account proposals. . . .

Clearly, the worker would have seen a significant decline in accumulated assets during the market declines of 2001–2002 and 2008–2009. However, despite these losses, the worker would always be better off than if he or she had received Social Security's rate of return. Thus, even if the worker had retired at the nadir of the decline, private investment would have out-performed Social Security. Moreover, while the accumulation would not yet have returned to its 2005 high, most of the losses would have been recouped by subsequent market gains.

What would this mean in terms of actual retirement benefits? The accumulation in the individual's account was used to purchase a lifetime annuity. With a life annuity such as Social Security, the retiree can never outlive the monthly income. A 6 percent charge was assessed as the cost of annuitization. . . .

Social Security benefits are calculated using the Social Security administration's "benefits calculator," with the ultimate wage in each scenario used as the last earned wage in the preceding year, and assume that full Social Security benefits are paid in the future, without change.

In every case, a worker would have received higher monthly benefits from private investment than from Social Security. In fact, even in the worst-case scenario, a low-wage worker who invests entirely in bonds, the worker does no worse than Social Security. . . .

Risk Factors

By its nature, private capital investment contains a degree of risk. The returns on stocks and bonds can obviously go down as well as up. Opponents of personal accounts have suggested that this means, *ipso facto*, that seniors would be left in poverty.

Of course, traditional Social Security is not without its own risks. Already the Social Security system provides a rate of return well below historic rates of return from private market investment. Moreover, the system cannot pay the promised level of benefits given current levels of revenue. Since Social Security benefits are neither guaranteed nor contractual, those benefits are almost certain to be reduced in the future. Workers who chose to invest privately, rather than rely on traditional Social Security, would therefore be exchanging the political risks of an under-funded Social Security system for the market risks of private investment.

A fair comparison of actual investment returns over the past 40 years to the benefits provided under Social Security shows that a system of private investment will, in fact, provide significantly higher rates of return than the current Social Security system, meaning that the vast majority of younger workers would be better off switching to such a system.

While there are limits to this type of analysis, it clearly shows that the argument that private investment is too risky compared with Social Security does not hold up. With Social Security running a cash-flow deficit today and facing a $21 trillion shortfall in the future that will make it impossible for it to pay promised benefits, private investment and personal accounts should be part of any discussion about reforming the troubled system.

Social Security Is a Wage Replacement Insurance Program, Not an Investment Program

Nancy J. Altman

Nancy J. Altman is the chairman of the board of directors of the Pension Rights Center, a nonprofit organization dedicated to the protection of Social Security beneficiary rights. She also serves on other boards of directors and is the author of The Battle for Social Security: From FDR's Vision to Bush's Gamble *(2005).*

Misleading language and myths have littered the debate over Social Security. Here are a few:

Myth: Social Security is a victim of the aging baby boom, reflected in the ratio of workers to retirees, which used to be 16 to 1, is now 3 to 1, and in 2030, will be 2 to 1.

Reality: Today's projected deficit has nothing to do with the size of the baby boom or worker to retiree ratios. The 16 to 1 ratio is a meaningless factoid, plucked from 1950, a year when Social Security was expanded to cover millions of new workers. The ratio never influenced policy in the slightest. It is the kind of ratio experienced by all pension plans, public and private at the start when few workers have yet qualified for benefits; the 2 to 1 ratio is meaningful and does translate into higher costs, but those costs were addressed decades ago. Congress has enacted ten significant Social Security bills since 1950. Every enactment has taken into account the baby boom, and each has left the program in long-run actuarial balance. The most recent enactment was in 1983, when the program was in balance through 2057—the year the youngest boomers, those born in 1964, will turn 93. How social security went from a projected surplus through 2057, when most of the baby boom will be dead, to today's projected deficit involves a number of factors, mainly related to changes in assumptions about wage growth, productivity and disability rates. The change from surplus to deficit is totally unrelated to the number of baby boomers, as one would surmise. After all, no new baby boomers have been born since 1983.

Eliminating Social Security's projected deficit many decades away, is one of the easiest problems facing the nation.

Myth: Social Security is going bankrupt.

Reality: From all federal programs, Social Security has been singled out for alarmist claims about bankruptcy because it operates under the conservative principles of a balanced budget and long-range projections. Bankruptcy is a meaningless concept when applied to the federal government or any of its programs. It is instructive to note that the bankruptcy language would disappear instantly if Congress simply reinstated the authorization, present in the law from 1943 to 1950, to pay any shortfall in Social Security out of general revenue.

Myth: Social Security is unworkable in the face of an aging population

Reality: Eliminating Social Security's projected deficit many decades away, is one of the easiest problems facing the nation. I propose a plan, which solves the deficit without benefit cuts, while raising extremely moderate taxes on just six percent of the workforce. More fundamentally, our economy can support our elderly, the widespread demographic anxiety notwithstanding. One measure of the ability of a population to support its nonworkers is the total dependency ratio, which is simply the sum of those under age 20 plus those age 65 and over divided by those ages 20 to 64. The lower the ratio, the lighter the burden. The total dependency ratio in the United States was highest in 1965. It has declined substantially since then and is not projected to reach that level again until around 2078. Moreover, the composition of the dependency ratio has changed. There are now more elderly and fewer children in the mix. This is a positive development from the perspective of income support. Very few five year olds can support themselves; many 70 year olds can and do.

Myth: Social Security won't be around when younger workers retire.

Reality: All the hype about bankruptcy has caused many to believe they are likely to receive no benefits from Social Security. Even if no change in Social Security is enacted for the next 75 years, future retirees will still receive higher benefits, in real dollar terms, than their parents who retire today. After all, for the next 75 years and beyond, Social Security will continue to collect billions of dollars in income week in and week out.

Myth: Social Security is a bad deal for younger workers. They would do better with private accounts.

Reality: Social Security provides more benefits than private accounts would. In addition to retirement benefits, young workers and their families have valuable life and disability insurance right now. Social Security includes features, such as complete protection against inflation, not offered in the private market. Further, Social Security has substantially lower administrative costs—returning more than 99 cents of every dollar collected—than private accounts are projected to have. Moreover, Social Security permits parents of young workers to live independently from their adult children and frees those children to focus their assets and attention on their own children.

Myth: Social Security is unfair to African Americans.

Reality: Social Security is vitally important to African-Americans. Social Security is the only source of retirement income for four out of 10 African-Americans, aged 65 and over. Without Social Security, the poverty rate among African-American seniors would triple, from 21 to 60 percent.

It is true that because of their shorter life expectancies, African Americans collect Social Security's retirement benefits, on average, for a shorter period of time than their European-American counterparts. But Social Security also provides benefits in the event of disability or death. Because of their poorer health status, blacks are more likely to become disabled or die prematurely than their white counterparts.

In a world where the private pension system is in trouble, and where savings are at their lowest rate since the 1930s, Social Security's rock solid guarantee of a floor of protection in retirement is more necessary than ever.

While approximately 13 percent of the population is black, black children constitute 23 percent of the children receiving Social Security survivor benefits, and African Americans represent 17 percent of those receiving disability insurance. Moreover, Social Security's benefits are progressively structured. Because African Americans have lower median earnings than the population as a whole and have higher rates of unemployment, they receive disproportionately higher benefits from Social Security.

Myth: Social Security is out-of-date, made for the Depression, and in need of modernization.

Reality: Social Security was enacted during the Depression, but it was not made for the Depression. The 1935 legislation provided that withholding from pay for Social Security would become effective on January 1, 1937. In order to give workers time to become insured, the 1935 enactment provided that monthly benefits were delayed, not due to begin for seven years after the 1935 enactment—until January 1, 1942, a date more than twelve years after the stock market crash of 1929.

President [Franklin] Roosevelt recognized that to get immediate assistance to people in need—to alleviate the immediate suffering caused by the Depression—there was no alternative to mean tested welfare. But for the long term—once the Depression was history and the economic health of the country was restored—the President wanted a system of insurance in place to guarantee for posterity that every American would have a reliable, stable source of income from which they could draw in old age. President Roosevelt's vision is as relevant and important today as it was then: As long as people are dependent on wages, Social Security is necessary. In a world where the private pension system is in trouble, and where savings are at their lowest rate since the 1930s, Social Security's rock solid guarantee of a floor of protection in retirement is more necessary than ever.

Myth: The President's private account proposal, allowing stock market returns, is designed to save Social Security.

Reality: If the issue were simply one of stock market returns, Social Security could be permitted to invest its reserves in the stock market. The issue is one of ideology, not investment strategy. Social Security is a wage-replacement program based on the insurance principle of pooled risk. Private accounts are private savings. Both can provide income in old age, but private accounts concentrate the risk while Social Security spreads it. . . . [President George W. Bush's] grandfather, Prescott Bush, who once remarked, "The only man I truly hated lies buried in Hyde Park," considered Franklin Roosevelt a traitor to his class. Roosevelt prevented his wealthy counterparts from saving for retirement solely on their own and instead forced them to pool a portion of their incomes with the rest of the population. The President [President Bush in 2008] appears determined to undo the work of his grandfather's nemesis. We should not allow him to use scare tactics and glib myths to undermine what remains the most successful domestic program in history.

Privatization Would Dismantle Social Security and Offer No Guarantees of Future Benefits

National Committee to Preserve Social Security & Medicare

The National Committee to Preserve Social Security & Medicare is a nonprofit, nonpartisan organization dedicated to providing a secure retirement for all Americans.

For 70 years the Social Security program has been protecting Americans against the loss of income due to retirement, death or disability. Over 157 million workers and their families are covered by their contributions to Social Security, and over 54 million Americans currently receive Social Security benefits.

Social Security is an enormously successful program which is essential to the retirement security of the vast majority of Americans. Social Security is the single largest source of retirement income. Two-thirds of Social Security beneficiaries receive over half their income from Social Security. For over 20 percent of retirees, Social Security is their only source of income. Without Social Security, 36 percent of the elderly would fall into poverty. Social Security provides a sound, basic income that lasts as long as you live.

Despite Social Security's continuing successes, the program is under attack by those who would like to privatize it. Some young workers are intrigued by the idea of diverting their payroll taxes into Wall Street accounts. Proponents of privatization promise ownership of accounts and big investment returns. They argue that Social Security is in a deep and immediate financial crisis that cannot be resolved without dismantling it and converting it into a system of market-based individual investment. To support their arguments, proponents of privatization have used misleading arguments about the nature of Social Security, the crisis facing it, and the value of converting Social Security to private investment accounts. Here are some of the myths and realties surrounding the Social Security debate.

Privatization results in huge cuts in Social Security benefits with no guarantee that private investment can replace lost benefits.

Myths and Realities

Myth 1: Privatization is a plan to save Social Security.

Reality: Privatization isn't a plan to save Social Security. It is a plan to dismantle Social Security. Private accounts do nothing to address Social Security solvency. In fact, because private accounts are financed by taking money out of Social Security, privatization nearly doubles Social Security's funding gap and moves forward the date of its insolvency.

Myth 2: Returns from private accounts will make up for the cuts in Social Security benefits.

Reality: Privatization results in huge cuts in Social Security benefits with no guarantee that private investment can replace lost benefits. Most plans would reduce guaranteed Social Security benefits over time, even for those people who do not choose a private account. For those who opt for a private account, benefits would be reduced even further.

Myth 3: Private account assets can be passed along to one's heirs.

Reality: Privatization leaves little to be passed on to one's heirs. Many plans would force account holders, upon retirement, to use the assets in their private accounts to purchase, at a minimum, an annuity sufficient to raise their total remaining Social Security benefits and monthly annuity payments to a poverty level income. The remaining assets in the account could then be used during retirement to make up for the plan's huge cuts in Social Security benefits. Only the excess after required annuitization and after expenses of retirement would be available to pass on to one's heirs. This is likely to amount to very little.

Myth 4: Private accounts are voluntary.

Reality: Private accounts may be voluntary, but the cuts are not. Even for those people who choose not to participate in a private account, Social Security benefits would be cut. Those cuts would effectively transfer money from those who opt out of accounts to those who opt in, forcing workers who decide against exposing themselves to the risks of Wall Street to subsidize those who are more willing to gamble with their retirement.

Social Security is a successful program that will be able to pay benefits for decades to come.

Myth 5: Privatization will exempt retirees and near retirees.

Reality: Retirees and near retirees should not count on being exempt. Because privatization diverts some of the employee-paid Social Security tax away from Social Security and into private accounts, Social Security's financial status is worsened and benefits for every retiree are threatened. In order to continue to pay benefits to retirees, privatization plans would require the Treasury to borrow trillions of dollars over several decades, causing an already huge federal deficit to balloon. This will increase the debt burden on all Americans, forcing policy makers to consider cuts in all federal programs, including Social Security.

Myth 6: Younger workers will receive a higher rate of return under a privatized system.

Reality: Younger workers are likely to realize little advantage from plans to privatize Social Security. That is because younger workers will have to pay twice—once to fund the benefits of current retirees under Social Security's pay-as-you go system and a second time to fund their own individual accounts. The Congressional Budget Office concluded that the costs of the transition to a privatized, prefunded system would reduce the rate of return on today's young people, the transitional generation, to a level lower than the rate of return on Social Security.

The Realities About Social Security's Solvency

Social Security is a successful program that will be able to pay benefits for decades to come. This year [2012] Social Security has an accumulated surplus of $2.7 trillion. Social Security will have sufficient reserves to pay benefits until 2036. Even after 2036, there will be enough money to pay 77 percent of the benefits owed, according to the Social Security actuaries.

The Social Security program's assets are held in the safest investment available—U.S. government securities. Those securities are legal obligations of the U.S. to pay principal and interest to the holder of the bonds. The securities have the same status as U.S. government bonds held by any other investor, including individual Americans and pension funds, and the Social Security Trust Fund has a legal obligation to pay full benefits as long as it has the funds to do so. . . .

Many myths and misconceptions have contributed to the belief that Social Security is in imminent danger and that Social Security privatization is the answer. Nothing could be further from the truth. The reality is that Social Security will continue to provide millions of retirees a sound, stable retirement. It may require some modest adjustments over a period of time, but it does not face an insurmountable crisis requiring major structural changes. Privatization, on the other hand, will unravel Social Security's important insurance protections, force huge cuts in benefits, increase risks to retirees, and force the Treasury to borrow trillions of dollars to fund the transition to the privatized plan. Social Security has been providing Americans a secure retirement for three quarters of a century. With sensible action it can continue to provide that security for decades to come.

Private Retirement Plans Could Not Provide the Same Benefits That Social Security Does

Louis Woodhill

Louis Woodhill writes about economic issues and is a frequent contributor to Forbes, *a business magazine.*

In 2005 George W. Bush put Social Security reform at the top of his domestic policy agenda for his second term as president. His initiative went down in flames. Six years later, Democrats are still making political hay with charges that Republicans want to "privatize Social Security."

Experts on the right periodically trot out analyses that show that workers would be better off if they could invest their payroll taxes in private retirement accounts. The public isn't buying their arguments, and the public is right. Major changes would have to be made in the economy before privatization of Social Security would be workable. Until and unless those changes are made, the public will continue to reject both the concept of Social Security privatization and candidates for office that advocate it.

Advocates of Social Security privatization typically note that if the average worker was allowed to invest the Social Security payroll taxes paid by him and his employer in a 401k account earning (historically) average returns, he would enjoy a much higher monthly income over the course of an average retirement than that afforded by Social Security. While this is true, it is also irrelevant.

For better or worse, Social Security combines a retirement plan with several welfare programs.

The public looks at Social Security as the foundation of retirement security.

People who work just enough to qualify for Social Security benefits get very high payouts relative to their contributions. This comes at the expense of other workers, who are forced to accept lower benefits than their contributions would otherwise justify. Also, the Disability Insurance (DI) element of Social Security is increasingly becoming an "early retirement" program for people who could work but would prefer not to.

Unless the nation is prepared to eliminate the "welfare" aspects of Social Security, it would not be possible to allow workers to invest all of their payroll taxes in their own private retirement plans. However, this is not the biggest problem that the public sees with Social Security privatization.

The public looks at Social Security as the foundation of retirement security. Its role is to be something that a worker can absolutely count on to keep him out of destitution if all else fails. Its role is not to offer an "upside," but to eliminate the "downside."

Because of this, Social Security cannot be compared with a 401(k); it can only be compared with a private plan possessing a similar risk profile. Social Security is the ultimate low-risk retirement program. If a worker lives to be 125, it keeps paying. If the price level doubles over five years, its benefits are fully indexed for inflation. And, Social Security is perceived to have no risk of default.

Accordingly, a private replacement for Social Security would have to take the form of a fully-inflation-indexed annuity with zero risk of default. Under present circumstances, the private markets cannot offer annuities of this kind, at least not at the scale required to replace Social Security.

Right now, a private entity wishing to offer a retirement plan that was directly comparable to Social Security would have to invest its assets in a "ladder" of TIPS [Treasury Inflation-Protected Securities]. This is the only investment that could provide inflation and default protection comparable to that provided by Social Security.

While in theory common stocks provide inflation protection, a replay of the 17-year period between 1965 and 1982 (during which the Dow lost more than 68% of its CPI-adjusted real value) would bankrupt a retirement plan that depended upon the stock market. A private retirement plan that aimed to directly replace Social Security could not afford to take such a risk.

Right now, there are not enough TIPS outstanding to support privatization of Social Security. And even if there were enough, right now 30-year TIPS are paying only 1.78% (and 5-year TIPS are yielding -0.61%!). Out of the meager yield from a "ladder" of such bonds, a private retirement plan would have to pay its administrative costs and generate a profit. Many analysts have criticized the poor returns promised by Social Security, but under current circumstances, it would not be possible for a private plan offering the same risk profile to do any better.

Considered strictly as a retirement plan, with both its "welfare" elements and the taxes that pay for them separated out, Social Security possesses advantages that it would be difficult or impossible for any private company to match. For one thing, when necessary, it can borrow at Treasury rates, something no private entity can do. For another, its sheer size keeps its administrative costs very low. However, Social Security's biggest competitive advantage flows from the asset side of its balance sheet.

The Social Security payroll tax (12.4% of payroll up to a "cap," currently $106,800) is structured in such a way that it reliably captures about 4.6% of GDP while having the least possible impact upon the rate of economic growth. Accordingly, the real asset of Social Security is not the so-called "Trust Fund," but the present value of its share of future GDP.

Right now, no private investment can duplicate the characteristics of Social Security's "asset." It enjoys default and inflation protection that only TIPS can match. However, the return on Social Security's "asset" is equal to the growth rate of real GDP, which can (and should) be much higher than the interest rate on TIPS. Over the past 100 years, the U.S. economy has grown at a real annual rate of more than 3.5%.

At the long-term average annual real economic growth rate assumed by the Social Security Trustees of 2.1%, Social Security has a large "unfunded liability", and would eventually run out of money to pay promised benefits. In their 2010 report, the Social Security Trustees estimated of the "present value to the infinite horizon" (PVIH) of this unfunded liability at $16.1 trillion, or 1.2% of future GDP.

No matter what economic policies were adopted, it would be very difficult for any private plan to match Social Security's ability to provide risk-free annuity income.

A small increase in economic growth (to about 2.5%) would eliminate Social Security's unfunded liability. More importantly, at real growth rates above the real interest rate on Treasury debt (which is estimated by the Trustees at 2.9%), the PVIH of future GDP is infinite, and so is the value of Social Security's "asset" (4.6% of infinity is infinity). A retirement plan with assets possessing infinite value would be difficult to compete with.

Because of the nature of Social Security's "asset," the best way to assure its long-term solvency is to increase the rate of economic growth. Cutting benefits and/or raising the retirement age is a distraction (and, for Republicans, a distraction that is potentially politically lethal).

The worst possible "solution" to the problems of Social Security (and therefore the one being pushed by some Democrats) would be to eliminate the "cap" on the wages subject to Social Security taxes. This would increase marginal tax rates on high earners by 12.4 percentage points, which would devastate economic growth. A tiny reduction in the long-term real economic growth rate would reduce the PVIH of Social Security's "asset" by far more than any possible tax hike could increase it.

If the dollar were stabilized by defining its value in terms of gold, the financial markets would stabilize, as would the economy. With no risk of inflation or liquidity-crisis-induced market crashes, partial privatization of Social Security might eventually become feasible. However, no matter what economic policies were adopted, it would be very difficult for any private plan to match Social Security's ability to provide risk-free annuity income.

Rather than trying to "reform" or privatize Social Security, Republicans should focus on assuring its long-term solvency via policies that increase the rate of economic growth. This is the right course, financially, economically, and politically. The public knows this, and it would be a good thing if the Republicans figured it out.

CHAPTER 4

How Should Social Security's Fiscal Issues Be Fixed?

Chapter Preface

In 2010, President Barack Obama appointed a commission to study the nation's fiscal status and make recommendations for reform in order to achieve fiscal sustainability over the long run. Called the National Commission on Fiscal Responsibility and Reform, and sometimes referred to as the Debt Commission, this body was made up of eighteen members, both Democrats and Republicans. The president appointed six members, including co-chairs Erskine Bowles (a Democrat) and Alan Simpson (a Republican), and the remaining twelve commission members were chosen by Senate and House leaders. One of the issues studied by the commission was Social Security, and in its December 2010 report, the commission issued a series of recommendations that called for major changes in the Social Security system to remedy its fiscal weaknesses.

In its report, the commission prefaced its recommendations on Social Security by noting its importance as a program that provides economic security for millions of Americans. This critical safety net must be maintained, the commission said, to fulfill Social Security's mission—to prevent people who can no longer work from falling into poverty. However, due to the fact that Americans now live much longer than those in the 1930s when the program was created, what began as a program to provide retirement income only for people close to the end of their expected lifespan has developed into a program that provides security for the last twenty years of life. This fact, the commissions explained, along with demographic changes caused by the large baby boom generation reaching retirement age, requires reform of the Social Security system to keep it fiscally sound. To accomplish this goal, the commission offered what it called a balanced plan of recommendations that requires all Americans to do their part.

The first recommendation offered in the commission's report was to make Social Security more progressive by curbing benefits for high income workers. Under this plan, benefit levels for people earning high incomes would gradually be lowered over several decades. Under the current system, Social Security retirement benefits are calculated using a formula that offers individuals 90 percent of their first $9,000 of average lifetime income, 32 percent of their next $55,000, and 15 percent of their remaining income, up to the taxable maximum. The commission recommended changing this to a four-level system that would eliminate the $55,000 level and substitute two new levels: $38,000 and $63,000. The commission's plan would then slowly change the replacement rates for these four levels. Under the new benefit formula, as of 2050, beneficiaries would receive 90 percent of the first $15,000 of income, 30 percent of income up to $63,000, 10 percent of income up to $102,000, and 5 percent of remaining income up to the taxable maximum.

Another commission recommendation designed to cover expected tax deficits was an increase in retirement eligibility ages. Under the current law, depending on the year of birth, retired workers can claim full Social Security benefits at age sixty-five to sixty-seven and reduced benefits for early retirement at age sixty-two. After the normal retirement age becomes sixty-seven for everyone in 2027, the commission suggested indexing the retirement age to increases in life expectancy, so that the normal retirement age would automatically increase to sixty-eight in 2050 and sixty-nine in about 2075. The early retirement age would similarly increase to sixty-three and sixty-four in those years.

Other cost-saving measures favored by the commission were gradually increasing the maximum wage level taxed for Social Security and using a more accurate measure of inflation to calculate Social Security Cost of Living Adjustments (COLAs). As of 2013, the taxable maximum wage cap was set at $106,800, with increases planned for the future, but the commission proposed increasing this amount so that 90 percent of all wages are taxed—a reform that would result in a taxable maximum of about $190,000 by 2050. The commission recommended using the chained consumer price index (CPI) for COLAs, a measure that takes into account what products consumers are buying.

The commission report also included several recommendations to increase benefits for certain citizens and make Social Security more flexible. In order to reduce poverty, the commission suggested that minimum-wage workers who work for thirty years be given a new minimum benefit of 125 percent of the poverty line in 2017, with increases indexed to wages thereafter. For very old retirees—those over eighty-five years of age—the commission would add a twenty-year bump up that would increase benefits by 5 percent after they had collected Social Security benefits for twenty years. Plus, the commission report suggested allowing beneficiaries to collect half their benefits as early as sixty-two and the other half at a later age, with a hardship exemption for those who are physically unable to work past age sixty-two but who cannot qualify for disability benefits. In addition, the commission would eliminate a loophole that allows people to collect early retirement benefits and then later withdraw that claim and return benefits without interest. The commission's other recommendations would require all states and localities to include their employees for Social Security coverage and direct the Social Security Administration to provide more information to citizens about their retirement options and the importance of personal retirement savings, since Social Security was never designed to be the sole source of retirement savings.

The commission's report, however, was never approved by the supermajority of commission members required for a formal endorsement. It also was never introduced for an up or down vote in either house of Congress. Instead, legislators from both parties and commentators from both the left and right criticized the report, some arguing that the Social Security cuts were too harsh and others claiming that more cuts should be made in entitlement programs. The result is that as of the summer of 2012, Congress had taken no action to fix Social Security's fiscal issues. The commentators in this chapter explain and discuss many of the reforms recommended by the Debt Commission.

Raising Eligibility and Retirement Ages Would Be One Way to Reduce Future Fiscal Imbalances in Social Security

Congressional Budget Office

The Congressional Budget Office is the main congressional agency responsible for reviewing congressional budgets and legislation with budgetary implications.

Raising the ages at which people can begin to collect Medicare and Social Security benefits would be one way to reduce long-term fiscal imbalances. The Congressional Budget Office (CBO) [a federal agency that advises Congress on fiscal matters] projects that, under current policies, federal outlays will significantly exceed federal revenues during the coming decade and beyond. Outlays for the government's two largest domestic programs, Social Security and Medicare, provide benefits primarily to the elderly. Those outlays are projected to increase rapidly because of the retirement of the baby-boom generation and growth in per capita spending for health care that is expected to continue to exceed growth in per capita gross domestic product (GDP) [a measure of the country's total economic output] over the long term. Unless policymakers decrease spending from projected amounts, increase revenues well above their historical average as a share of GDP, or adopt some combination of those two approaches, federal debt will become unsustainable.

Congressional Budget Office, "Raising the Ages of Eligibility for Medicare and Social Security," Issue Brief, January 2012, pp. 1–2.

Three Categories

This [viewpoint] analyzes the effects of raising the ages at which most people become eligible to collect benefits under those two programs. Three categories of eligibility could be involved in such a change:

- The Medicare eligibility age (MEA), currently 65;

- The early eligibility age (EEA) under Social Security, at which participants may first claim retirement benefits, currently 62; and

- The full retirement age (FRA) under Social Security, at which participants are eligible to receive full benefits, currently 66 but scheduled to increase to 67 for people who were born after 1959.

Effects of Eligibility Changes

Raising the MEA or the FRA would reduce federal spending on benefits and affect potential beneficiaries in various ways. For example, if the MEA rose to 67, annual federal spending on Medicare would be reduced by about 5 percent, CBO estimates, because most people would lose access to Medicare at ages 65 and 66. A small share of those people would end up without health insurance, CBO expects, but most would have insurance coverage through employers, other government health care programs, or other sources. Many of the people who lose access to Medicare would pay higher premiums for health insurance, pay more out of pocket for health care, or both. An increase in the FRA amounts to a benefit reduction; raising the FRA to 70, for example, would ultimately reduce Social Security outlays by about 13 percent, CBO estimates. Raising the EEA would have a much smaller effect on the federal budget in the long term: It would delay access to benefits for many people, but their monthly benefit amounts would be higher.

Raising the ages of eligibility for Medicare and Social Security also would induce people to work longer. A two-year rise in the EEA or a three-year rise in the FRA would boost both the size of the labor force and total output of the economy by slightly more than 1 percent, CBO estimates. Raising the MEA by two years would probably result in much smaller increases in the size of the labor force and total output.

Under a schedule of gradual increases in all three eligibility ages that is described below, CBO estimates that by 2035, outlays for Social Security and Medicare would fall by 0.4 percent of GDP and federal revenues would rise by around a half percent of GDP—leading to a reduction in the budget deficit of nearly 1 percent of GDP, not including the effects of lower interest outlays. CBO estimates that the outlay effects would grow to about 1 percent of GDP in 2060, when all retirement benefits would be based on the higher FRA, and the revenue effects would grow to about three-fourths of a percent of GDP in that year. Altogether, the federal budget deficit would be reduced by about 1 3/4 percent of GDP in 2060.

Social Security Should Be Strengthened by Removing the Cap on High Incomes

Bernie Sanders

Bernie Sanders is an independent senator representing the state of Vermont.

Social Security is the most successful social program in American history. It shouldn't be privatized; its benefits shouldn't be cut; and the retirement age shouldn't be raised.

Before Social Security was established 75 years ago, more than half of our elderly population lived in poverty. Because of Social Security, the poverty figure for seniors today is less than 10%. Social Security also provides dignified support for millions of widows, widowers, orphans and people with disabilities.

Since it was established, Social Security has paid every nickel it owed to every eligible American, in good times and bad. As corporations over the last 30 years destroyed the retirement dreams of millions of older workers by eliminating defined-benefit pension plans, Social Security was there paying full benefits. When Wall Street greed and recklessness caused working people to lose billions in retirement savings, Social Security was there paying full benefits.

The Attack on Social Security

Despite its success, Social Security faces an unprecedented attack from Wall Street, the Republican Party and a few Democrats. If the American people are not prepared to fight back, the dismantling of Social Security could begin in the very near future.

Rep. Paul D. Ryan (R-Wis.), the new chairman of the House Budget Committee, wants to partially privatize Social Security, lower its cost-of-living adjustments and drastically cut benefits. An increasing number of his fellow Republicans agree. Rep. Michele Bachmann (R-Minn.), one of the leaders of the "tea party" movement, has said that we need to "wean" everyone except current retirees off Social Security and Medicare.

Many young Americans have been convinced that when they reach retirement age, Social Security will not be there for them.

There are threats on other fronts. A deficit-reduction commission established by President [Barack] Obama called for increasing the retirement age to 69, reducing cost-of-living adjustments for today's retirees and deeply reducing benefits for future retirees who make as little as $42,000 a year.

Just about every day, one conservative or another tells us that Social Security is in crisis, that it is going bankrupt and that the Social Security Trust Fund contains nothing more than a pile of worthless IOUs. As a result of this barrage of misinformation, many young Americans have been convinced that when they reach retirement age, Social Security will not be there for them.

The Need to Maintain and Strengthen Social Security

So what are the facts?

According to the latest report of the Social Security Administration, the program will be able to pay all of its promised benefits for the next 26 years. After 2037, Social Security will still be able to pay about 78% of promised benefits.

The nonpartisan Congressional Budget Office has come to a similar conclusion: Social Security will be able to pay full benefits to every eligible recipient until 2039, and after that, it will be able to cover 80% of promised benefits.

Although Social Security will be strong for more than a quarter-century, Congress should strengthen it for the longer term. That is why I agree with the president, who has called for raising the cap on taxable income. Today [February 2011], that cap is at $106,800; no matter how much money you make, Social Security taxes are only deducted on the first $106,800. But by removing the cap on incomes of $250,000 or more, we can make Social Security fully solvent for generations to come.

Even with no change, the fact is that Social Security has a $2.6-trillion surplus that is projected to grow to more than $4 trillion in 2023. Is this surplus, as some have suggested, just a pile of worthless IOUs? Absolutely not!

Social Security invests its surpluses, as it should, in U.S Treasury bonds, the safest interest-bearing securities in the world. These are the same bonds that wealthy investors and China and other foreign countries have purchased. The bonds are backed by the full faith and credit of the U.S. government, which in our long history has never defaulted on its debt obligations. In other words, Social Security investments are safe.

Further, despite the manufactured hysteria about a crisis, Social Security has not contributed one penny to the very serious deficit situation the United States faces. Social Security is fully funded by the payroll tax that workers and their employers pay; it's not paid for by the Treasury. Our deficit has been, in recent years, largely caused by the cost of two wars, tax breaks for the rich, a Medicare prescription drug program written by the insurance and pharmaceutical industries, and the Wall Street bailout—not Social Security.

Why has there been such a concerted effort to privatize Social Security, raise the retirement age or cut benefits? First, Wall Street stands to make billions in profits if workers are forced to go to private financial establishments for their retirement accounts. Second, as the Republican Party has moved far to the right and become more anti-government, there are more and more Republicans who simply do not believe government has a responsibility to provide retirement benefits to the elderly, or to help those with disabilities.

Needless to say, I strongly disagree with both of those propositions. In my view, maintaining and strengthening Social Security is absolutely essential to the future well-being of our nation. For 75 years it has successfully provided dignity and support for tens of millions of Americans. Our job is to keep it strong for the next 75 years.

Want to Fix the Economy? Start With Social Security

Peter Diamond

Peter Diamond is a professor emeritus at the Massachusetts Institute of Technology in Cambridge, Massachusetts, and was a co-recipient of the Nobel Prize in Economics in 2010 and a consultant to the US Congress about Social Security reform in 1974.

With millions of Americans out of work, a mounting federal debt, and the national economy at risk of a renewed recession, no one seems to be thinking about the Social Security system at the moment. But they should be. Fixing Social Security—that is to say, restoring the program's actuarial balance—would serve our economic needs in a number of ways. It would help with our long-term fiscal problems without damaging our short-run outcomes; moreover, it would be a lasting commitment, not a seeming fix that might be undone. Most importantly, it's something that our existing political system might actually accomplish.

In contrast to fixing Social Security, addressing now the budgetary elephant in the room, healthcare costs, has little to recommend it. We don't sufficiently understand how to make health care work better. We do understand how to shift costs from the federal government, but that does not address the root of the problem. We have a healthcare cost problem not only for the federal budget, but also for state and local budgets, for businesses and for individuals. In short, we have a system that doesn't work well. While there are some changes we should make now, learning how to fix it thoroughly is going to take experimentation, evaluation, and repeated corrections. Not to mention the fact that we have a history of some of the cost-lowering legislation in the health care sector getting canceled later. Tax reform has a similar history of some backtracking; a number of the important 1986 tax reforms have already been rolled back.

There's a pretty good track record for Social Security reform.

Social Security, by contrast, is both easy to understand, and already has a history of significant, positive, lasting reforms. The program's design is simple: it's essentially money in and money out. Everybody who looks at it understands how it works. We also can estimate, with fairly good accuracy, what sort of behavioral changes—and cost savings—would be produced by changes in the program's parameters.

Moreover, restoring Social Security's actuarial balance makes eminent macroeconomic sense. It would have a significant effect on the debt held by the public in the long run, without harming the economy in the short run. For example, the reform that Peter Orszag and I proposed in our book *Saving Social Security* would have reduced debt held by the public by 25 percent of GDP [gross domestic product, a measure of the nation's total economic output] within 45 years of its enactment.

It's encouraging, as well, that there's a pretty good track record for Social Security reform. The last major reform of Social Security came in 1983, and it looks likely to have given us 50 years of ability to pay scheduled benefits. None of its major provisions have been rolled-back, not even the controversial increase in the age for full benefits from 65 to 67. In fact, Social Security has a long history of addressing future concerns with sustainable policies: Future payroll tax rate increases were incorporated into the program from the very beginning. While these increases were sometimes delayed and sometimes accelerated, they were never canceled. Even now there's largely a consensus on how to approach fixing Social Security: Everyone agrees that we should phase changes in slowly, thereby having no negative short-run effects. In short, if we fix Social Security, we are very unlikely to undo it.

And with the system's trust fund reserves projected to run out in 2036, pretty much everyone agrees that we do have a Social Security problem, and would have one even if we didn't have a debt or overall deficit problem. Starting in 2036, the payroll tax revenue will continue to flow in but will be enough to pay only three-quarters of scheduled benefits. With no legislated change, benefits would need to be cut by a quarter.

In some ways the current political climate makes this an especially good time to try fixing Social Security. Fixing Social Security involves some combination of raising taxes and lowering benefits, both of which are very hard to legislate until the public feels it's facing an imminent crisis. Heightened concerns among many Americans about the long-run debt held by the public should help cultivate acceptance for changes in Social Security.

One issue that has held up reform is the dispute between Republicans and Democrats over whether to use existing payroll tax revenues for individual savings accounts. I suspect that idea is no longer much in play—not least because diverting payroll tax revenues from Social Security's existing trust fund to individual accounts with diversified portfolios would add to public debt. The reason for that is simple: Instead of the trust fund using payroll tax revenues for the purchase of government debt, some revenue would instead go to individual purchases of stocks and corporate bonds, resulting in more debt that gets sold to the public and so more risk of a negative bond market reaction and a greater cost if one does happen. For example, the proposal from the [George W.] Bush administration would have added 19 percent to the debt to GDP ratio by 2050. And some proposals would have had massive increases—the proposal by Congressman Paul Ryan and then-Senator John Sununu would have added more than 90 percent to the debt to GDP ratio by 2050.

The hard issue is what mix to have between additional revenues and decreased benefits. To get the 1983 Social Security reform, President [Ronald] Reagan and Speaker of the House Tip O'Neill agreed that the mix would be 50/50, and they set up a committee to work out the details. Congress stayed fairly close to that balance, if not exactly on it. Finding an acceptable mix remains a serious problem and policymakers will need to find a mechanism for addressing it.

The base-closing commissions remain a prime example of Congress partially tying its own hands in order to get an improved result, an example that a lot of analysts now want to use. Following that example, a Social Security commission's report (with a sufficient majority) would receive special congressional rules requiring an up-or-down vote and disallowing the use of a filibuster. To make this work Congress should legislate instructions to the commission requiring a particular balance between direct revenue increases and benefit cuts. (Any increase in the maximum earnings subject to tax or coverage of state and local workers would increase both revenues and benefits and should be treated as a separate category). Unlike much of the legislation discussed in Washington, the public should be able to relatively easily follow the Social Security debate, and what it would mean to refuse all revenue increases or to refuse all benefit cuts for the program. Neither position is politically viable for a plan to rescue Social Security and polls have repeatedly shown that the public wants a balanced Social Security reform.

Social Security reform—with its large contribution to the long-run debt problem—should not be seen as exclusive, but combined with the sort of large infrastructure program that could stimulate the economy. As with Social Security, there is wide agreement that we have major infrastructure needs throughout the country, and fixing now what we would otherwise need to fix later would not really add to the long-run debt level. In fact, current infrastructure spending would have a lower real cost by drawing in part on otherwise idle labor and capital as well as having a multiplier effect on unemployment.

But while reforms to Social Security would ideally be combined with this kind of fiscal stimulus, at a time of rising polarization, policymakers should at least address those problems that we know we can fix. Social Security is the place to start.

A Mix of Minor Changes Would Fix Social Security

Philip Moeller

Philip Moeller is a contributing editor to U.S. News & World Report Money, *a business and financial magazine.*

Every time I write about the financial condition of Social Security, I get incredibly angry at Congress and the White House. They should step up to the plate and apply the relatively minor financial changes that would restore the program to complete financial sustainability. Next to the truly tough issues of healthcare spending, federal deficits, and taxes, Social Security is a walk in the park.

Governments seem to do little right these days, at a time when the public desperately needs to see something positive from its elected leaders. Restoring the public's confidence in the staying power of Social Security would send a positive message to younger generations. They now have ample reason to doubt they will receive benefits that are anything like those being paid to current retirees.

A Valuable Program

The value and success of this program are not in question. More than 55 million Americans draw benefits today. Some 14 million of them are so dependent on Social Security that they would be impoverished without its payments—payments they have largely (although not entirely) funded with their own payroll taxes.

As the values of private investment accounts were tanking after the Great Recession [December 2007–June 2009], Social

Security proved the benefit of a dependable retirement program. It was there when we needed it, and with modest changes, it can continue to be there for current and future generations.

We're talking about heading off a 25 percent spending shortfall more than two decades away.

The Social Security Administration spends about $12 billion a year and employs about 80,000 people to run all its retirement and disability benefit programs. Those are big numbers, but not compared with the much larger profits that private companies charge for running 401(k)s, IRAs, and other private retirement accounts. Social Security is a bargain in terms of its administrative costs.

Minor Issues

Putting Social Security on firm financial footing for the next 50 or 75 years is not hard because the program's issues are not huge. This week's [April 25, 2012] annual Social Security trustee report said the program would be unable to pay full benefits in the year 2033, three years earlier than projected in the same report last year.

Even so, if nothing was done, Social Security could pay its full benefits for 21 more years and then still be able to pay 75 percent of those benefits after that. So, we're talking about heading off a 25 percent spending shortfall more than two decades away.

Still, 20 years is not far off in terms of gradually implementing changes that would provide for the program's longer-term needs while not forcing jarring changes on people already retired or within 10 years of retiring. The program's smaller disability insurance component is only four years from insolvency, in case lawmakers need a match lit under them sooner.

Lastly, the options for dealing with Social Security's financial needs have been studied to death and then some. There are few surprises here. And there aren't serious ideological issues either, at least not by comparison with the intractable tax-and-spend tug of war that has paralyzed Congress of late. But compromises would be needed.

The three most prominently advanced reforms are to reduce the size of the annual cost of living adjustment, raise the retirement age, and lift the ceiling on earnings subject to payroll taxes. It's now at $110,100 a year, but because high earners have fared so well in recent years, the program taxes a smaller percentage of the nation's wage income than it used to.

The Simpson-Bowles deficit restructuring plan of late 2010 included these and other suggested Social Security reforms. They provide a well-researched starting point for changing the program. The Social Security components of that plan could be peeled off, introduced separately, and subjected to extensive House and Senate hearings.

If Congress and the White House were serious, the program could be put on solid financial ground again well before the elections. And because Social Security has historically been separate from the rest of the federal budget, its needs could be addressed without opening up that much bigger can of worms.

The common wisdom is that no major issue will be addressed in Washington before the November elections. I get it. It's sad, really, that there is not more heat on legislators to act. Perhaps we've just become too accustomed to gridlock. But wouldn't it send a wonderful message if legislators actually demonstrated that they cared more about doing the public's business than results of their next election? Helping Social Security would set the table for those tougher spending and tax decisions. I am, of course, terminally naive. But wouldn't it be great!

Social Security Benefit Cuts Should Be Concentrated on High-Income Beneficiaries

Allan Sloan

Allan Sloan is editor at large for Fortune, *a business and financial magazine.*

Well, there's at least one virtue to the depressing numbers that Social Security's trustees unveiled last week [April 25, 2012]—they prove that I was right. In February I wrote that the system's finances had deteriorated badly, due largely to the energy price boosts created by the Arab Spring. And so they have: Those increases were the primary factor in Social Security's inflation adjustment hitting 3.6 percent this year rather than the 0.7 percent baked into the trustees' 2011 report. That added significant costs to Social Security, but little or nothing in the way of added revenue to help offset them.

Now that the gloomy numbers are official, people belatedly are pointing with alarm to the projections that Social Security's cash expenses will exceed its cash income as far as the eye can see.

By contrast, last year, the trustees projected positive cash flow for several years, which would have given the system a little breathing space.

Being a born contrarian, I won't join the gloom-and-doom crowd. Instead, I'll try to show you some numbers you haven't seen before about how important it is to fix Social Security the right way—and quickly—to avoid hurting the most vulnerable members of our society. And I will offer you hope, a commodity in rare supply these days.

Relevant Numbers

We will skip all that stuff about the Social Security trust fund (which has accounting and political significance but no economic significance) and go straight to the number that matters.

The Center for Economic and Policy Research calculated the impact of Social Security benefit cuts to various groups.

To wit: Last year, the Treasury had to borrow $160 billion to give to Social Security so that its checks (okay, its electronic deposits) wouldn't bounce. Even in an era of trillion-dollar budget deficits, that's serious cash. The borrowing consisted of $103 billion to cover the cost of the "holiday" reducing employees' Social Security taxes, and another $57 billion to redeem Treasury securities that Social Security's trust fund cashed in.

This kind of borrowing can't be sustained indefinitely. So far, we haven't seen adverse effects on interest rates because the Federal Reserve is holding rates down by buying vast amounts of Treasury securities. But when the Fed stops doing that—which it will, sooner or later—big trouble will set in if we haven't cleaned up our act.

Protecting the Less Fortunate

These numbers are all familiar. Now, to numbers you've probably not seen. In a fascinating April report—okay, it's fascinating to numbers junkies, not to normal people—the Center for Economic and Policy Research calculated the impact of Social Security benefit cuts to various groups ranging from lower-income single people who don't own homes to the well-off (albeit not rich) likes of my wife and me, who own our home.

It did this by placing a dollar value on projected Social Security benefits, a good way to put the number in an overall wealth context.

I make out much better than a lower-income single non-homeowning person does if Social Security is cut across the board, say by increasing the retirement age. That's because even though any benefit reductions cost me more dollars than such a person because my benefits are higher, Social Security is a far smaller proportion of my net worth.

Social Security benefits represent a stunning 92 percent of the net worth of single non-homeowners whose income is in the bottom 80 percent of all Americans, according to this study, compared to 62 percent for married homeowners in the bottom 80 percent, and only 19 percent for those in the 80 to 99 percent bracket. (I'm in the top 2 or 3 percent bracket, which isn't broken out.)

So if we're going to cut benefits—which I think is inevitable—let's be careful to concentrate the impact on the likes of me (for whom Social Security is important, but not crucial) and mitigate the impact on the less fortunate.

Why do I think that's doable? Because the key players involved in its number crunching—who will ultimately design a plan—are people of good faith. Take Social Security's two public trustees—Chuck Blahous and Robert Reischauer—who span the right-wing left-wing political spectrum. You could see clearly at the report unveiling that they like and respect each other—even though they disagree. The world of Social Security techies, in which I've traveled for more than a decade, is full of people like Blahous and Reischauer.

So, I have faith that sooner or later—I hope sooner—it will finally occur to politicians that there's a huge downside to not fixing Social Security and having benefits cut by 25 percent in 20 years or so, if things continue on their current path. Once that happens, I think the faceless bureaucrats, many of whom I've come to know and like, will make a deal happen. And Social Security will be there for my children, none of whom currently expects to see a dime from it.

Social Security Reforms Must Achieve Both Solvency and Modernization

Howard Gleckman

Howard Gleckman is an author, a resident fellow at the Urban-Brookings Tax Policy Center, and a former senior correspondent in the Washington bureau of Business Week, *a leading financial magazine.*

Social Security has two obvious problems. While the system is not "broke," as some insist, it will have only enough money to provide future retirees with about three-quarters of their promised benefits. At the same time, it is poorly designed for the needs of a country where life expectancy and the nature of work and family have changed dramatically since Social Security was created in 1935.

As a result, those who most need social insurance—single women, low-wage workers, the disabled, and the very old—get much less than they need. On the other hand, those who need benefits least get the most.

If Washington policymakers could hold the twin goals of solvency and modernization in their heads at the same time, they could take a few relatively modest steps needed to reform Social Security—and enhance a key pillar of the social safety net for the most vulnerable elderly.

A Need for Common Sense Change

The trick will be to get past the dissonant squabbling that passes for debate these days. Conservatives need to recognize that Social Security will remain a defined benefit program for

Howard Gleckman, "Social Security: Fixing It Isn't Hard," *The Christian Science Monitor*, June 21, 2011. Copyright © 2011 by Howard Gleckman. All rights reserved. Reproduced by permission.

the foreseeable future. Liberals must overcome their fear that any change at all is the death knell for social insurance.

An extra year of work would solve about one-third of the program's funding problems.

While Social Security played a key part in reducing poverty rates among the elderly from more than one-third to less than 10 percent over the past half-century, the system is increasingly leaving some seniors behind. Just a few examples: Divorced and never-married women are three times more likely to be poor in old age than married women, and more than one-third of retired workers and widows get benefits that fall below the poverty level.

In this environment, AARP [American Association of Retired Persons] deserves tremendous credit for declaring its willingness last week [June 2011] to sit down and work out a Social Security deal. By doing so, it recognizes two essential realities: the seven decade old Social Security system needs to change, and it will.

But how can lawmakers and advocacy groups build a consensus with the dual aims of securing long-term solvency and modernizing the system? I think they can by agreeing to six common-sense principles:

1. *Create a respectable minimum benefit* for low-income workers, increase some widows' benefits, and create an additional benefit for the very old (say, 85 or older).

2. *Raise the retirement age,* including the minimum benefit age of 62. An extra year of work would solve about one-third of the program's funding problems. More and more of us can work into our 70s and a modern Social Security system should reflect that. It makes no sense for government to signal that we should stop working at 62 when we are likely to live for two more decades.

3. *Protect those who work physically demanding jobs.* While the percentage of older Americans who do manual labor is shrinking, those who do this work need to be protected. Long overdue reforms in Social Security's badly broken disability system would help.

4. *Increase contributions and reduce benefits for high-earners.* Everybody would still get some benefit—Social Security is not welfare and must retain its status as social insurance. But there is no reason why it can't be made more progressive.

5. *Preserve the defined benefit nature of Social Security.* Adding an additional savings component is a good idea. But the public is not interested in taking on additional risk with their retirement.

6. *Be absolutely transparent about benefits and structural changes.* Whatever Congress does, there should be no surprises. As it is, many young people have no confidence in Social Security. Reforms should restore their faith in this key piece of the old-age safety net. But government should also be clear that in the future Social Security will only supplement—and not replace—other retirement savings for middle- and upper-income retirees.

By following these principles, Congress and President [Barack] Obama could fix Social Security in a way that makes it both solvent and relevant to a 21st century world.

Organizations to Contact

The editors have compiled the following list of organizations concerned with the issues debated in this book. The descriptions are derived from materials provided by the organizations. All have publications or information available for interested readers. The list was compiled on the date of publication of the present volume; the information provided here may change. Be aware that many organizations take several weeks or longer to respond to inquiries, so allow as much time as possible.

AARP
601 E St. NW, Washington, DC   20049
(888) 687-2277
website: www.aarp.org

Formerly known as the American Association of Retired Persons, AARP is a nonprofit, nonpartisan membership organization that advocates on behalf of people age fifty and over. The group seeks to ensure that older Americans have independence, choice, and control over policies that are beneficial and affordable to them and society as a whole. A search of the AARP website produces a wealth of materials on the topic of Social Security; a few examples are: "Social Security State Quick Fact Sheets: 2012," "The Importance of Social Security and Medicare," and "Social Security: A Key Retirement Resource for Women."

Campaign for America's Future
1825 K St. NW, Suite 400, Washington, DC   20006
(202) 955-5665 • fax: (202) 955-5606
website: www.ourfuture.org

The Campaign for America's Future is a strategy center for organizations and individuals devoted to promoting progressive values such as accessible education, affordable health care, and secure retirements for all Americans. The group also advocates for clean energy, independence from Middle East oil, and restoration of a representative and responsible federal government. Social Security is a key progressive concern, and a search of the site for this topic produces a number of relevant publications. Examples include: "Making Sense: Social Security," "Speaking Truth About Saving Social Security," and "What Social Security Report Says vs. What They Tell You It Says."

Cato Institute
1000 Massachusetts Ave. NW, Washington, DC   20001-5403
(202) 842-0200 • fax: (202) 842-3490
website: www.cato.org

The Cato Institute is a think tank dedicated to libertarian principles such as individual liberty, limited government, free markets, and peace. Cato conducts research on various policy issues, including Social Security. The group's website contains a section on this topic that addresses issues such as reform ideas, Cato's proposed solutions, international social security reforms, the value of personal savings accounts, and Social Security's financial crisis. The website is a rich source of conservative articles and studies relevant to Social Security. Publications include "Bankrupt: Entitlements and the Federal Budget," "Still a Better Deal: Private Investment vs. Social Security," "Higher Taxes or Smaller Entitlements: What Should Voters Choose?"

Center on Budget and Policy Priorities (CBPP)
820 1st St. NE, Suite 510, Washington, DC   20002
(202) 408-1080 • fax: (202) 408-1056
e-mail: center@cbpp.org
website: www.cbpp.org

The Center on Budget and Policy Priorities (CBPP) works on fiscal policy and public programs that affect low- and moderate-income families and individuals. CBPP research and analysis is designed to encourage policymakers to develop policy options to alleviate poverty in the United States. One research area is Social Security, and the CBPP website provides numerous articles and analyses on this subject, including topics such as Social Security's accomplishments, fiscal status, and reform proposals. Publications include: "What the 2012 Trustees' Report Shows About Social Security" and "Contrary to 'Entitlement Society' Rhetoric, Over Nine-Tenths of Entitlement Benefits Go to Elderly, Disabled, or Working Households."

The Heritage Foundation
214 Massachusetts Ave. NE, Washington, DC   20002-4999
(202) 546-4400
website: www.heritage.org

The Heritage Foundation is a conservative think tank that promotes public policies based on the principles of free enterprise, limited government, individual freedom, traditional American values, and a strong national defense. One of the group's issues is retirement security, and its website is a source of many research papers and articles on the Social Security program. Publications include, for example, "Entitlements Policy in 2012 Elections," "2012 Report: Social Security Finances Much Worse," and "The Real Cost of Public Pensions."

National Committee to Preserve Social Security
& Medicare (NCPSSM)
10 G St. NE, Suite 600, Washington, DC
(202) 216-0420 • fax: (202) 216-0446
e-mail: webmaster@ncpssm.org
website: www.ncpssm.org

The National Committee to Preserve Social Security & Medicare (NCPSSM) is an advocacy organization that seeks to prevent the dismantling of Social Security, Medicare, and Medicaid programs. The group believes that these programs are critical to the nation's income and health security. The NCPSSM website offers a number of publications, such as "Social Security Primer," "Truth Booklet," "Federal Income Security," "Direct Deposit of SS Benefits," and "Women and SS Benefits."

National Organization for Women (NOW)
1100 H St. NW, Suite 300, Washington, DC   20005
(202) 628-8669
website: www.now.org

The National Organization for Women (NOW) consists of feminist activists in the United States, with five hundred thousand contributing members and 550 chapters in all the states and the District of Columbia. NOW's goal is to promote equality for all women, and one of the group's important issues is Social Security. The NOW website contains a section on this topic that includes informative publications such as "Basic Statistics on Social Security and Women," "NOW Statistics Fact Sheet," and "Don't Make Us Work 'Till We Die!" The website is also a source for useful news articles on Social Security.

Pew Research Center
1615 L St. NW, Suite 700, Washington, DC   20036
(202) 419-4300 • fax: (202) 419-4349
website: http://pewresearch.org

The Pew Research Center is a nonpartisan "fact tank," which provides information on the issues, attitudes, and trends shaping the United States and other countries. It conducts public opinion polls and social science research, reports on and analyzes news, and holds forums and briefings, but it does not take positions on policy issues. A search of the Center's website produces several publications on public attitudes about Social Security, entitlement reform, and deficit spending. Examples include: "Public Wants Changes in Entitlements, Not Changes in Benefits" and "Baby Boomers Approach Age 65—Glumly."

Bibliography

Books

Daniel Béland

Social Security: History and Politics from the New Deal to the Privatization Debate. Lawrence: University Press of Kansas, 2005.

Daniel Béland and Alex Waddan

The Politics of Policy Change: Welfare, Medicare, and Social Security Reform in the United States. Washington, DC: Georgetown University Press, 2012.

Andrew G. Biggs

Social Security: The Story of Its Past and a Vision for Its Future. Washington, DC: AEI Press, 2011.

Charles Blahous

Social Security: The Unfinished Work. Stanford, CA: Hoover Institution Press, 2010.

Jim Blankenship

A Social Security Owner's Manual: Your Guide to Social Security Retirement, Dependent's, and Survivor's Benefits. Charleston, SC: CreateSpace, 2011.

Andy Landis

Social Security: The Inside Story. Charleston, SC: CreateSpace, 2012.

Eric Laursen

The People's Pension: The Struggle to Defend Social Security Since Reagan. Oakland, CA: AK Press, 2012.

Frederick R. Lynch — *One Nation under AARP: The Fight over Medicare, Social Security, and America's Future.* Berkeley: University of California Press, 2011.

Carmelo Mesa-Lago — *Reassembling Social Security: A Survey of Pensions and Health Care Reforms in Latin America.* New York: Oxford University Press, 2012.

Mitchell A. Orenstein — *Privatizing Pensions: The Transnational Campaign for Social Security Reform.* Princeton, NJ: Princeton University Press, 2008.

Jonathan Peterson — *Social Security for Dummies.* Hoboken, NJ: John Wiley & Sons, 2012.

George E. Rejda — *Social Insurance and Economic Security.* Armonk, NY: M.E. Sharpe, 2011.

William A. Seymore — *The Truth About Social Security: Almost Everything You've Been Told About Social Security Is Wrong.* Bloomington, IN: Xlibris, 2011.

Allen W. Smith — *The Looting of Social Security: New Release of the Book They Didn't Want You to Read.* Winter Haven, FL: Ironwood, 2010.

Joseph F. Stenken — *2012 Social Security & Medicare Facts.* Erlanger, KY: National Underwriter, 2012.

US Government   *Social Security Handbook 2010:*
                 Overview of Social Security Programs.
                 Blue Ridge Summit, PA: Bernan
                 Press, 2010.

Periodicals and Internet Sources

Binyamin   "Even Critics of Safety Net
Appelbaum and   Increasingly Depend on It," *New York*
Robert Gebeloff *Times*, February 11, 2012.

David L. Faust   "Reader: Social Security Should Not
                 Be Privatized," *Lewistown Sentinel*,
                 March 8, 2012.

Trip Gabriel   "A Gingrich Alternative to Social
                 Security," *New York Times*, November
                 21, 2011. http://thecaucus.blogs
                 .nytimes.com.

Iris Greene   "Why Social Security Is Important to
                 You," *Daily Courier*, October 18,
                 2010.

Paul Krugman   "How Important Is Social Security?"
                 New York Times, August 30, 2008.
                 http://krugman.blogs.nytimes.com.

D. Krunner   "Why Social Security Is
                 Failing—Social Security History and
                 Issues," InfoBarrel, October 17, 2010.
                 www.infobarrel.com.

Merrill Matthews "What Happened to the $2.6 Trillion
                 Social Security Trust Fund?" *Forbes*,
                 July 13, 2011.

Laura Meckler — "Washington Wire: Is Social Security a Ponzi Scheme?" *Wall Street Journal*, September 8, 2011. http://blogs.wsj.com.

Rick Moran — "Social Security Disability Fund Is Nearly Broke," *American Thinker*, August 22, 2011. www.americanthinker.com/blog.

New York Times — "Room for Debate: Is Social Security a Ponzi Scheme?" September 9, 2011. www.nytimes.com.

Ted Nugent — "Social Security Is a Ponzi Scheme, Only Worse," *Washington Times*, September 21, 2011. www.washingtontimes.com.

Dawn Nuschler — "Social Security Reform: Current Issues and Legislation," Congressional Research Service, September 14, 2010. http://aging.senate.gov/crs/ss6.pdf.

Barack Obama — "Barack Obama's Statements on Social Security, Speech to the AARP Convention on the COLA and the Retirement Age," Campaign for America's Future, September 6, 2008. www.ourfuture.org.

Robert Powell — "If You're Under 40, Don't Bank on Social Security," *Wall Street Journal*, April 28, 2012.

Robert J. Samuelson	"Let Them Go Bankrupt, Soon: Solving Social Security and Medicare," *The Daily Beast*, May 22, 2009. www.thedailybeast.com.
Michael Tanner	"Yes, It Is a Ponzi Scheme: In Fact, Social Security Is a Bit Worse than That," *National Review*, August 31, 2011. www.nationalreview.com.
Derek Thompson	"Social Security Is Really Important! (But So Is Almost Everything Else)," *The Atlantic*, May 17, 2011. www.theatlantic.com.
Cynthia Tucker	"Social Security Should Not Be Privatized," ajc.com, February 21, 2011. http://blogs.ajc.com.
Paul N. Van de Water	"Off the Charts: No, Social Security and Medicare Aren't Going 'Bankrupt,'" Center on Budget and Policy Priorities, April 25, 2012. www.offthechartsblog.org.
Wall Street Journal	"Private Accounts Can Save Social Security," May 2, 2011.

Index

A

Afghanistan, 99
African Americans
  social security fair to, 116–117
  social security needs of, 51–52, 57–58
  social security not fair to, 89
Aid to Dependent Children program, 16–17
Aid to the Blind, 21
Aid to the Elderly, 21
Aid to the Permanently and Totally Disabled, 21
Altman, Nancy J., 114–118
American Association of Retired Persons (AARP), 154
Arab Spring, 149
Argentina, 64, 91
Asignación Universal por Hijo, 64
Australia, 91, 101

B

Baby boom generation, 23–24, 48, 91, 93
Bachmann, Michele, 138
Barrientos, Armando, 65–66
Bernstein, Jonathan, 72
Blahous, Charles, 41, 151
Bolivia, 65
Bolsa Familia, 64
Borowski, Julie, 87–89
Boskin, Michael, 81
Bowles, Erskine, 130
Brazil, 64
Bush, George W.
  debt to GDP ratio, 143–144

ownership society philosophy, 95
  Personal Benefits Statement, 73
  private accounts, 91
  social security failures, 107
  social security reform, 18, 101, 107, 124
  tax cuts by, 59
Bush, Prescott, 118

C

Cambodia, 65
Carney, Tim, 88–89
Carter, Jimmy, 33
Cato Institute, 89, 109
Center for American Progress, 77
Center for Economic and Policy Research, 150
Center on Budget and Policy Priorities, 53–59, 61
Children and social security, 56
Child Support Grants (South Africa), 65
Chile, 91, 101, 102, 106
China, 65
Cichon, Michael, 63, 64
Clinton, Bill, 91, 101
CNN/ Opinion Research Corp. poll, 40
Colombia, 65
Committee on Economic Security (CES), 16–17
Congressional Budget Office, 33, 122, 134–136, 138
Consumer price index (CPI), 132
Corporate pensions, 61